STAND
on the
WORD
Study Guide

PAUL'S PRISON LETTERS

EPHESIANS
PHILIPPIANS
COLOSSIANS
PHILEMON

A 14-Day Journey through the Word

with Tony Perkins

FAMILY RESEARCH COUNCIL
SINCE 1983

FIDELIS PUBLISHING ®

ISBN: 9798999024657

Paul's Prison Letters: Ephesians, Philippians, Colossians, Philemon
A Stand on the Word Study Guide

Content contributor: Dr. Kenyn Cureton
Cover design: Diana Lawrence
Interior layout design/typesetting: Lisa Parnell
Copyediting: Lisa Parnell

Order at www.faithfultext.com for a significant discount.
Email info@fidelispublishing.com to inquire about bulk purchase discounts.

Fidelis Publishing, LLC Sterling, VA • Nashville, TN
www.fidelispublishing.com

Manufactured in the United States of America

10 9 8 7 6 5 4 3 2

FIDELIS
PUBLISHING

Contents

Map: Paul's Journey to Rome / iv

Day 1. Paul's Prison Letters: An Introduction....................1

Map: Paul's Second Missionary Journey / 5

Day 2. Ephesians 1....................7

Day 3. Ephesians 2....................15

Day 4. Ephesians 3....................21

Day 5. Ephesians 4....................29

Day 6. Ephesians 5....................37

Day 7. Ephesians 6....................45

Day 8. Philippians 1....................53

Day 9. Philippians 2....................63

Day 10. Philippians 3....................71

Day 11. Philippians 4....................79

Map: Colossae at the Time of Paul's Imprisonment / 86

Day 12. Colossians 1–2....................87

Day 13. Colossians 3–4....................97

Day 14. Philemon....................111

Appendix 1. Stand on the Word Bible Reading Plan........119

Appendix 2. Prayer: Talking with God....................121

Appendix 3. How to Share Your Faith....................127

Appendix 4. The Solution to Our Greatest Challenge......133

Notes....................138

Paul's Journey to Rome

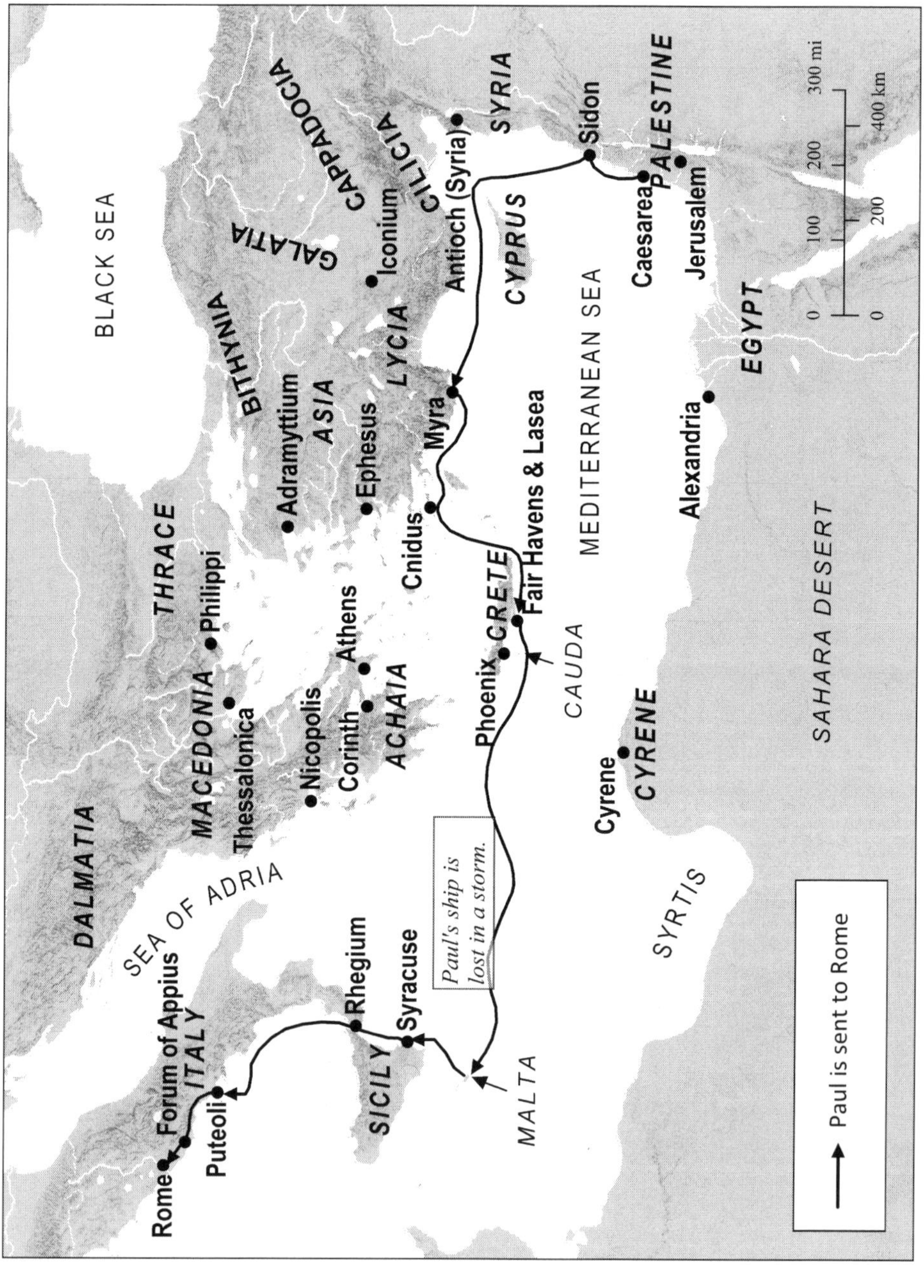

— Day 1 —

Paul's Prison Letters: An Introduction

Welcome to the Stand on the Word Study Guide on *Paul's Prison Letters*. I begin with some questions: How can you take your stand for Christ while incarcerated? How do you find joy in Jesus while in jail? How can you praise God while in prison? How can you exalt Christ as preeminent and preach freedom in His name while in chains? The apostle Paul gave us the answers to those questions and much more in four letters written while he was incarcerated, chained to a Roman guard. In fact, Paul mentioned his imprisonment in each of the letters (see Ephesians 3:1; 4:1; Philippians 1:13; Colossians 4:3, 18; Philemon 1:10).

Speaking of incarceration, several notable Christian leaders have written significant works from prison. I think of John Bunyan, who wrote his classic *The Pilgrim's Progress* while imprisoned. Then there is the renowned German pastor, Dietrich Bonhoeffer, jailed by the Nazis in Tegel Prison then executed, but his writings were later published as *Letters and Papers from Prison*. Also, famed civil rights leader Rev. Dr. Martin Luther King Jr. penned his impactful *Letter from Birmingham Jail* while in prison. Yet most famous of all are these New Testament letters the apostle Paul wrote during his house arrest in Rome.

The timeframe for these writings is around AD 61–62, and that lines up with the end of the book of Acts. Remember, Paul had journeyed to Jerusalem, guided by the Holy Spirit there (20:22–23) despite the warnings of the prophet Agabus and others that arrest and imprisonment awaited him (21:4, 10–12). After reaching Jerusalem and conferring with James and the apostles (21:17–26), Paul went up to the temple to worship, was identified by some of the disgruntled Jews from Roman Asia, was arrested on trumped-up charges, and was nearly killed by the mob (21:2–36). He then appeared before the Sanhedrin, and they nearly tore him apart (22:30–23:10). Providentially, Paul survived a plot to take his life (23:12–22) and then was transferred to prison in Caesarea (23:23–35). He faced a couple of hearings before Roman and Jewish authorities, and ultimately, he appealed to Caesar because he was a Roman citizen (chaps. 24–26). Consequently, Paul was put on a ship full of prisoners bound for Italy, and God providentially preserved him through shipwreck and venomous snakebite (chaps. 27–28). Ultimately, Paul reached the end of his journey: Rome, the capital of the empire. There he was placed under house arrest for two full years, awaiting his trial before Caesar (chap. 28).

Though his arrival in Rome was not like Paul had envisioned when he wrote to the Roman believers (see Rom. 15:22–24), everything had played out exactly as God had planned. For this extended season, Paul was no longer free to travel from city to city, sharing the gospel and planting new churches. He was stuck in one place. Again, Paul was literally chained to a Roman guard. Yet God even used Paul's incarceration to further His sovereign plans and purposes. The result? The Spirit of God led Paul to write these four amazing letters to the churches in Ephesus, Philippi, Colossae, and to a slaveowner named Philemon—letters we continue to read and find in them instruction, encouragement, and hope even today.

How to Get the Most from the Study Guide

While the study guide offers spiritual insights and applications, the real impact comes from the words of Scripture, which is the Word of God. Please read the selected text for the day in your own Bible. God's Word is "living and powerful" (Heb. 4:12). The Spirit of God uses His Word to change your life. Nothing else can do this. So before reading the daily commentary, read God's Word!

In fact, here are five habits to cultivate as you approach God's Word each day:

1. *Read it through:* Don't skip around. Read the entire selection of Scripture. If you are pressed for time, please read the Bible before you read the study guide notes. So read it through.
2. *Think it over:* Meditate on it. Let it marinate in your mind. If you can, take notes. We provide a notes page at the end of each day. Think it over.
3. *Pray it in:* Personalize the Scripture. Turn the verse that speaks to you into a prayer and then pray it into your life. Ask God what you need to do in response. This leads to the next habit.
4. *Live it out:* Consider ways to apply what God is revealing to you and ways you can obey Him. Put His Word into practice. Make it a part of who you are, how you think, how you speak, and how you behave toward God and other people. In other words, take God's Word and live it out.
5. *Pass it on:* Don't keep it to yourself. People are in your life who need the same truth God has spoken to you in His Word. Share it. Pass it on.

About Stand on the Word

Stand on the Word is a ministry of Family Research Council, whose mission is to serve in the kingdom of God by championing faith, family, and freedom in public policy and in the culture from a biblical worldview. The purpose of Stand on the Word is to lay the foundation for a biblical worldview through daily reading and application of God's Word. For the daily journey, we have created a chronologically prioritized reading plan through the entire Bible that can be accessed at frc.org/Bible, by texting the word *Bible* to 67742, or by downloading the Stand Firm app.

Paul's Second Missionary Journey

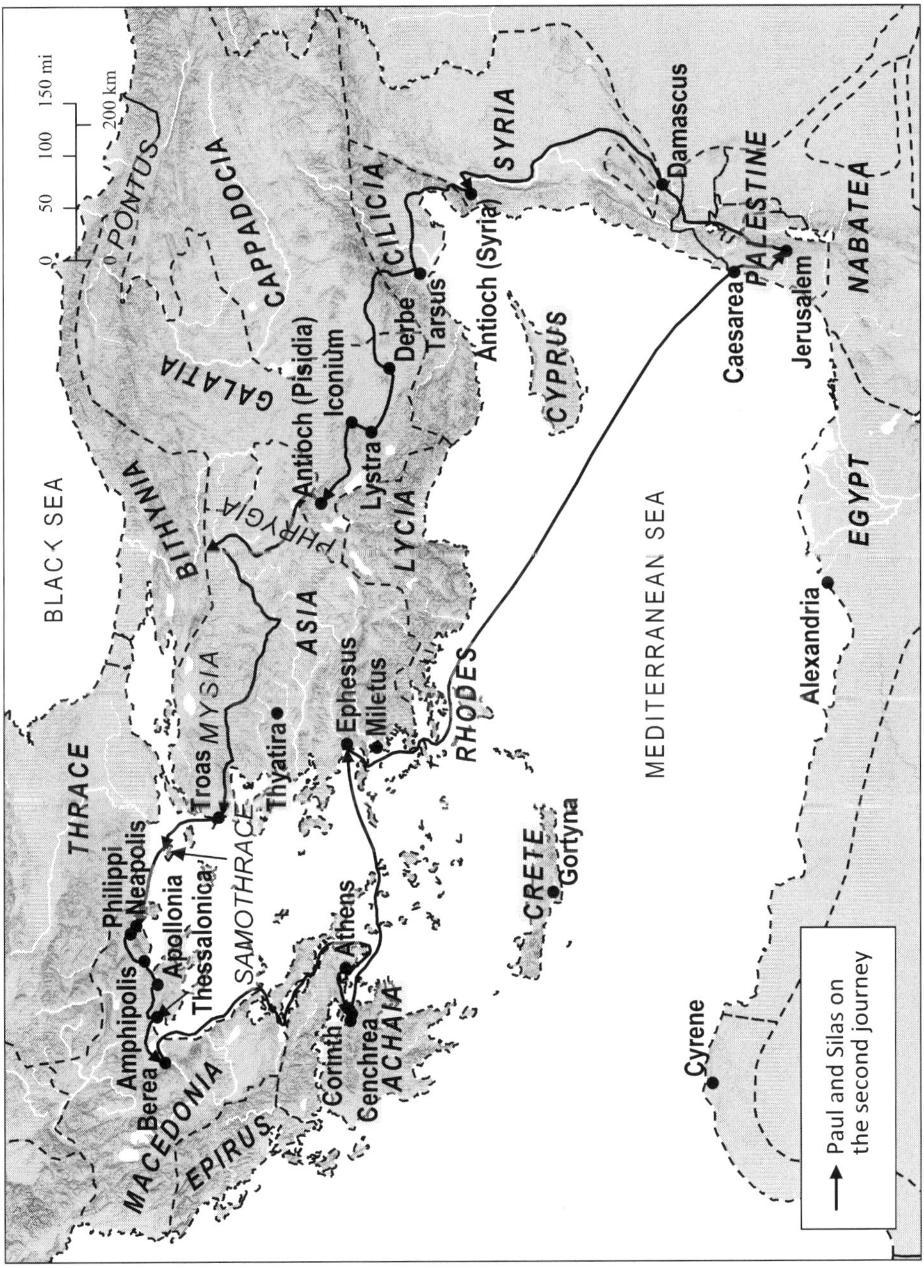

— Day 2 —

Ephesians 1

Verse of the Day

> And He put all things under His feet, and gave Him to be head over all things to the church, which is His body, the fullness of Him who fills all in all.
>
> — *Ephesians 1:22–23*

Please read the entire Scripture selection in your own Bible and highlight or underline verses that stand out to you and write down insights before you read the observations and engage the questions below.

Today we begin our study of Ephesians, which is certainly one of the most important writings of Paul, who is universally accepted by credible New Testament scholars as the author. The letter to the churches in Ephesus is one of my favorite sections of Scripture. In fact, this letter contains my life verse: "Therefore take up the whole armor of God, that you may be able to withstand in the evil day, and having done all, to stand" (6:13). Before we dive into our study of the text, let's consider the background and a brief overview of Ephesians.

Background

Ephesus was the capital of Asia Minor, so it was a political center—in fact Rome had made it a free city. It also was a religious center. The temple of the goddess Diana, or Artemis, was located there and is one of the seven wonders of the ancient world. Underneath the statue was one of the largest bank vaults of the day. So, the city was a financial hub, and all kinds of trade flowed in and out, by the river and roads by which goods were brought in from the interior to the busy harbor from which they were shipped out. Business was booming. GDP was strong. Consequently, Ephesus was not only a political and religious center; it was also a commercial center. Multiplied thousands of people from all over crowded its streets.

Ephesus also became a strategic place in the spread of the gospel, and God led Paul to start a church there. All told, Paul stayed a total of nearly three years according to Acts 19–20. In the early years, Priscilla and Aquila labored there. The eloquent Bible teacher Apollos was converted and ministered in Ephesus. Paul's apprentice in the ministry, Timothy, also spent time there. Apparently, John the apostle served as pastor of the church until he was taken away during the persecution and exiled on Patmos. And the first letter from the risen Lord to the seven churches in Revelation is addressed to Ephesus. So it was a strategic city, and its church was a significant work. It is not surprising Paul felt compelled by the Spirit of God to write to the believers in Ephesus while he was in prison in Rome sometime around AD 60–62.

Overview

Unlike Paul's letters to the Thessalonians, Galatians, Corinthians, and Philippians, the letter to the Ephesian believers is on the other end of the spectrum when it comes to Paul sharing personal information or addressing specific problems. This is a big-picture letter. Paul divided it into two clear segments: (1) the doctrinal section on the foundation of the church in chapters 1–3 and (2) the practical section on the function of the church in chapters 4–6.

In the first part, Paul contended that through faith in Christ we are placed in corporate solidarity with Christ. In fact, he repeatedly referred to believers as being "in Christ." As a result, the believer's position as having been chosen, elected, predestined, and so on, by God can only be understood in light of our union with Jesus, who was chosen by God and predestined before the foundation of the world to die as a sacrificial substitute, be raised in triumph, and is now at the right hand of God. And because of this union, Paul said believers are raised from spiritual death with Christ by the mercy of God and even now are seated in the heavenlies in Christ (2:4–6). This positional truth is all a result of God's grace by means of our faith (2:8–9).

Paul's focus was not only on the individual in Christ but also on the body of believers, the church, and its foundation. Ephesians, perhaps more than any other New Testament book, presents the purpose and plan of God for this body, the church. The first three chapters describe God's purpose from eternity past to create a holy community, chosen in Christ, adopted as sons and daughters of God—Jews and Gentiles alike. And now this mystery of the ages has been revealed in how the gospel brings this diverse group into a unified church.

Ephesians 4:1 provides the hinge of the letter: "I, therefore, the prisoner of the Lord, beseech you to walk worthy of the calling with which you were called." After laying out profound theological truths in the first half of the book, in chapters 4–6, Paul challenged the Ephesians and all believers to apply the positional truths of the first three chapters to practical living. Consequently, in these three chapters, Paul moved from the foundation of the church to the function of the church. Specifically, he addressed how we are to live out these lofty truths in our relationships within the church, in the home, at work, and in the world. In the final chapter, Paul addressed the spiritual dimension of the battle in which we are engaged and encouraged believers to be strong in the Lord and in the power of His might, prayerfully putting on God's armor. He then concluded with the call to stand and keep on standing. In fact, this is the theme of the letter and of my life: Keep Standing!

Commentary

Again, this first chapter of Ephesians covers the foundation of the church and the revelation of God's plan. Our key verses, which basically summarize the chapter, are Ephesians 1:22–23: "And He put all things under His feet, and gave Him to be head over all things to the church, which is His body, the fullness of Him who fills all in all." Before the foundation of the world, God had a plan to redeem humans from sin for the purposes of God's own glory. This is really the essence of this first chapter, and three points look at the revelation of God's plan.

The first point is the *plan* of God from eternity past. We see this in verse 4a where Paul said, "just as He chose us in Him before the foundation of the world." God's plan was not plan B because of unforeseen complications with humankind. This was the plan of a sovereign, all-knowing, and all-powerful God. This was His plan, and it's what He revealed to Paul. And it's what Paul said is revealed in Christ Jesus.

God's plan is for us to be holy and without blame in a relationship with Him. God wants us to be in a relationship with Him, and this comes through Jesus Christ by His grace. His grace saves us. His love is demonstrated through sending His Son, and in and of itself, this was an act of grace. But that unmerited favor from God offers us forgiveness and redemption that comes from receiving Jesus Christ, His death on the cross, His burial, and His resurrection. So this is the plan of God.

The second point is the *purpose* of God. In the first few chapters, this is the mystery revealed in Christ Jesus that Paul talked about. So what is the purpose of God? It's all for the glory of God. It's *His* glory. This is really not about us. In the church today, we tend to make this about us. It really isn't. Yes, we are the beneficiaries of God glorifying Himself, but it's not, as one of the more popular praise choruses claims, that God did not want heaven without us. This sounds nice. And while we're grateful God sent His Son to die for us, ultimately, it's not about us.

While we think we should be at the center of God's world, the reality is that God should be at the center of *our* world. God's plan and purpose certainly includes us, but the focus shouldn't be on us. In the end it is about God. The purpose is to bring God glory. Even when Jesus came to this earth, He said, "Not My will, but Thy will be done." Why? Because it was about the glory of the Father. We see this in Ephesians 1:6a, which says, "to the praise of the glory of His grace." And we see it in verses 12 ("that we who first trusted in Christ should be to the praise of His glory") and 14 ("who is the guarantee of our inheritance until the redemption of the purchased possession, to the praise of His glory"). This is about the glory of God. That's what His purpose is about.

The third and final point is the *provision* of God. Here's where the benefits come. We are the beneficiaries of His love and grace that Christ Jesus demonstrated. The provision of God is there to accomplish His plan and the purpose of bringing glory to Himself.

This means, in part, He does that by providing us with every spiritual blessing, and I see seven spiritual blessings in this passage.

1. *God chooses us.* We don't go looking for God. God comes after us and chooses us. I'm not going to get into the subjects of predestination or foreknowledge because they are deep subjects. But here's what we do know without question: God chooses us. He adopts us as sons and daughters.
2. *God redeems us and accepts us through Jesus Christ.* He cleanses us, forgives our sins, and accepts us into fellowship with Him through Jesus Christ.
3. *God revealed the mystery of His will.* Ephesians 1:11 says, "In Him also we have obtained an inheritance, being predestined according to the purpose of Him who works all things according to the counsel of His will." This is revealed in the Old Testament era. They didn't have this understanding of what God was doing. God revealed this in Jesus Christ.
4. *God unifies us with other believers in Jesus Christ.* We're going to see more about this in the next chapter.
5. *God gives us hope and purpose.* We have purpose and meaning in this life through Jesus Christ. And this is part of the spiritual blessing. We're not here aimlessly wandering around, occupying space, and consuming air. We have a purpose. And what is this purpose? It is to glorify God and to enjoy Him forever.
6. *God gives us an eternal inheritance.* I want you to grasp these spiritual blessings we enjoy in this life. Of course, we must deal with persecution and opposition. But this is a down payment; it's just a precursor to the eternal inheritance that is ours in Christ Jesus. How do we know? Because we are

joint heirs with Christ. We are the recipients of the work of Jesus Christ, adopted as sons preparing to receive the eternal inheritance. How do we know this is going to happen? That leads us to the last point.

7. *God gives us the Holy Spirit as a seal.* He seals us. I know this is a doctrinal teaching some take issue with. I think we're sealed. I think once we truly accept Jesus Christ as our Lord and Savior, we are sealed by the Holy Spirit into the relationship as a son or as a daughter. He says in verse 14, "who is the guarantee of our inheritance until the redemption of the purchased possession, to the praise of His glory." Now, what does that mean? This is a nonrevocable down payment. It is a promise that the rest is coming. And so, the Holy Spirit is really the earnest payment that the inheritance, the fullness of our redemption and glorification, is coming.

So how do we know God can do this? Paul continued in verses 19–21: "and what is the exceeding greatness of His power toward us who believe, according to the working of His mighty power which He worked in Christ when He raised Him from the dead and seated Him at His right hand in the heavenly places, far above all principality and power and might and dominion, and every name that is named, not only in this age but also in that which is to come." Next time we move to Ephesians 2 and will look at God's revelation and His manifestation of grace, which is part of His plan.

Questions for Reflection and Discussion

1. What are the benefits of those who are "in Christ" according to Paul in chapter 1, and specifically how do we get there (see vv. 12–13)?

2. What did Paul pray that we would come to know (see vv. 15–22)?
   a. Hope to which God called us
   b. Riches of His glorious inheritance in the saints
   c. Immeasurable greatness of His power toward us who believe
   d. All the above

Notes on Today's Bible Reading

— Day 3 —
Ephesians 2

Verse of the Day

> For by grace you have been saved through faith, and that not of yourselves; it is the gift of God.
>
> —*Ephesians 2:8*

Please read the entire Scripture selection in your own Bible and highlight or underline verses that stand out to you before you read the observations and engage the questions below.

Ephesians 2 covers the revelation of God's grace. One of the more famous verses in all of Scripture, verse 8 captures the essence of this: "For by grace you have been saved through faith, and that not of yourselves; it is the gift of God." In fact, there are four key points in this pivotal chapter.

First, Paul talked about the default position of humankind: We are dead in trespasses and sin. And if left untreated by the antidote of God's grace administered through faith in Jesus Christ, this condition will result in the second death, which is eternal. That is our default position, but what does this look like?

Paul laid it out in the first part of the chapter. He said we're under the influence of the devil. Verse 2 describes him as "the prince of the power of the air, the spirit who now works in the sons of disobedience." That is the course of this age. That is the default position. Until the new covenant of grace, that was the general condition of all humankind after the fall. But someone might protest, "Just because you don't serve God doesn't mean you serve the devil. That's pretty harsh, isn't it?" Well, Jesus declared in Luke 11:23, "He who is not with Me is against Me, and he who does not gather with Me scatters." You see, we have only two choices: Either we serve God, or we serve the devil. That's what Jesus said.

The second point is the deliverance of God. Look what it says in Ephesians 2:4: "But God, who is rich in mercy, because of His great love with which He loved us." As we saw in chapter 1, God's plan, while we are the beneficiaries of the plan, is not only about us; ultimately it's about God's glory. And in this, it displays His nature and His character. So in saving us by His grace, unmerited favor, He displays His nature and His character because of His great love.

Notice Paul said, "God . . . is rich in mercy." Before we were even aware of our situation, where we were dead in our trespasses and sin, God took the initiative. Our salvation is the result of His initiative, not ours. That's important to note. We talked about this in chapter 1, the sovereignty of God. He chose us. He pursued us.

So, we see the default position of humankind, we see the deliverance by God, and third, we see the divine design of God firsthand. Ephesians 2:10 says, "For we are His workmanship, created in Christ Jesus for good works, which God prepared beforehand that we should walk in them." We are the products of God's grace. He wants to show us off as the products of His grace. We are produced through Jesus Christ, and we are prepared for good works. Notice that we're not saved *by* good works. Paul instead declared, "For we are His workmanship, created in Christ Jesus for good works"—not *by* good works, *for* good works—"which God prepared beforehand that we should walk in them." You see, once we're saved, once we are redeemed by God's grace, we are saved to do good works, to bring glory to God. Works don't save us. Rather, works are evidence of our salvation.

The fourth and last point is the destruction or dissolving of division. Note what Paul said in Ephesians 2:14–17: "For He Himself is our peace, who has made both one, and has broken down the middle wall of separation, having abolished in His flesh the enmity, that is, the law of commandments contained in ordinances, so as to create in Himself one new man from the two, thus making peace, and that He might reconcile them both to God in one body through the cross, thereby putting to death the enmity." What was Paul talking about? The separation between the Jews and the Gentiles and that Jesus Christ, the cross of Christ, brings us together.

Remember in the Old Testament, there was a covenant with the Jewish people, and Gentiles were on the outside. Even here, there's a reference made to the temple where there were the partitions, the "middle wall of separation," the court of the Gentiles. The uncircumcised could not go past that point. There was even a separation of the women and the men. Yet Paul declared that the walls have been demolished, "There is neither Jew nor Greek, there is neither slave nor free, there is neither male nor female; for you are all one in Christ Jesus. And if you are Christ's, then you are Abraham's seed, and heirs according to the promise" (Gal. 3:28–29). By His death, burial, and resurrection, Jesus makes us one family—heirs together of God's promise. In Christ, we are God's temple: His Spirit dwells in us, and we are "being built together into a dwelling place for God by the Spirit" (1 Cor. 3:16; 6:19; Eph. 2:21–22). This unity does not erase God-given distinctions; it removes any hierarchy when it comes to our inherent value and worth before God because every individual bears the image of God. Consequently, the ground is level at the foot of the cross, leaving no room in the church for pride, prejudice, or partiality.

As we wrap up our study, here are a couple of closing observations. The first is that religion divides. We see it all across the world the division caused by religion. I saw it personally when I served as the chairman of the US Commission on International Religious Freedom. Yet here is a second observation: Religion divides, but Jesus unites. When we accept God's plan of redemption through Jesus Christ according to His grace, He unites us. Through His Spirit, He makes us one. The world is not and cannot be made right by religion, but it can be made right by a relationship with Jesus Christ. And Paul laid out the foundation here in Ephesians 2.

Questions for Reflection and Discussion

1. How did Paul describe people in their unsaved condition, and how has God responded (see 2:1–5)?

2. As Paul explained it simply, how is it possible for a person to be saved (see v. 8)?
   a. It is by God's grace alone.
   b. Through faith in Christ alone
   c. It is God's gift alone—not our works.
   d. All the above

Notes on Today's Bible Reading

— Day 4 —

Ephesians 3

Verse of the Day

> [T]hat the Gentiles should be fellow heirs, of the same body, and partakers of His promise in Christ through the gospel.
>
> — *Ephesians 3:6*

Please read the entire Scripture selection in your own Bible and highlight or underline verses that stand out to you before you read the observations and engage the questions below.

The first three chapters of the book of Ephesians deal with doctrinal issues, the foundation of the church. Today we are discussing the final chapter of this doctrinal section, and the theme is the mystery revealed. Our key verse is Ephesians 3:6, "that the Gentiles should be fellow heirs, of the same body, and partakers of His promise in Christ through the gospel."

I want us to look at the revelation of the *mystery*. The word in the original language refers to a hidden truth. Specifically, Paul talked about things hidden in the counsel of God from before the beginning of time. So what is the mystery? Paul told us right here in verse 6: Both Jew and Gentile alike would come to faith and be incorporated into the same body through the grace of God that is extended through Jesus Christ.

As you know, some Gentiles in the Old Testament feared and followed the God of Israel. Yet there was a difference. In fact, you recall that they were separated in the temple. There was a court specifically reserved for the Gentiles. So, there was a barrier between Jew and Gentile. However, Jesus removed the barrier.

This was the mystery kept in the counsel of God from before the foundation of the world, that there was going to be this age of grace for the Gentiles to be saved and incorporated into God's family. Paul referred to it as "the fullness of the Gentiles" in Romans 11:25. When the Jewish people generally rejected Christ because of the hardness of their hearts, the gospel was offered to the Gentiles, and they were generally more receptive to it. Obviously, Paul's argument in Romans 9–11 is that this partial hardening of Israel to the gospel doesn't preclude individual Jews from being saved—after all Paul and the apostles were Jewish—but it prevented the nation from accepting Jesus as Messiah until God's plans for the Gentiles are complete. Indeed, when the time is right, God will restore the Jewish nation, and they will come to faith in Christ, ending "the fullness of the Gentiles" (see Isa. 17:7; 62:11–12; Rom. 11:26).

Back to Paul's point in Ephesians 3 and this mystery revealed. Through the gospel, God invites both Jews and Gentiles into the same body of believers, into the same fellowship, adopting them both as sons and daughters into His family. As we've talked about before, Paul said in Galatians 3:28, "There is neither Jew nor Greek, there is neither slave nor free, there is neither male nor female; for you are all one in Christ Jesus."

So that is the mystery, but how was it revealed? Let's look at Ephesians 3:5: "which in other ages was not made known to the sons of men, as it has now been revealed by the Spirit to His holy apostles and prophets." This mystery was revealed by the Holy Spirit, who came upon the church at Pentecost. Verse 9 tells us why God revealed this: "and to make all see what is the fellowship of the mystery, which from the beginning of the ages has been hidden in God who created all things through Jesus Christ." Here's the application: We are to be faithful stewards of this sacred secret, this mystery. Like Paul, we are to make known the offer of God's grace to Jew and Gentile alike. The old dispensation of the law, the old covenant, and the exclusivity of salvation being only for the Jewish people—with the Gentiles being excluded—is obsolete in light of the cross. Now there is a new covenant of grace. Not only Jews but also Gentiles are welcomed into God's kingdom by faith in Jesus Christ. So, this was the revelation of it, but it did more.

Look at Ephesians 3:10: "to the intent that now the manifold wisdom of God might be made known by the church to the principalities and powers in the heavenly places, according to the eternal purpose which He accomplished in Christ Jesus our Lord." This multifaceted, multisided, unsearchable wisdom of God was unveiled to both the angels of light and the angels of darkness through the church.

This was a key part of God's purpose. God was "schooling" the spirits through this new spiritual community united in Jesus. In fact, the apostle Peter told us the angels were curious about what God was doing (1 Pet. 1:10–12). As they say, "Inquiring minds want to know," and God even lets the angels, good and bad, in on it. He reveals the manifold, literally the multicolored, wisdom of God, speaking of its beauty and perfection, in His body, His church. So this is more of the revealing of the wisdom of God that is beyond searchable, incomprehensible to the human mind, but now revealed to men and angels alike.

Through this grace, through this mystery revealed, we can enter the fellowship of the mystery. But Paul said in Ephesians 6:19–20, "and for me, that utterance may be given to me, that I may open my mouth boldly to make known the mystery of the gospel, for which I am an ambassador in chains." So this unveiling of the hidden things in God, is what allows men, women, and children to understand that God loves them and we can have a relationship with Him through Jesus Christ. And what does it provide? What is this plan? What is this hidden thing? Look at Ephesians 3:12: "in whom we have boldness and access with confidence through faith in Him." This mystery revealed the ability to boldly access God through Jesus Christ. Why? Because our sins have been atoned for and we have been adopted as the sons and daughters of God into His family.

The second part of this chapter (vv. 14–21) is actually a prayer for the believers in Ephesus. Paul prayed for God to bless them according to the riches of His glory. And then we see in this chapter, Paul reminded us that the riches of God's glory are infinite. Sometimes in a land of plenty it is difficult to truly conceive of God's glorious riches.

This reminds me of several years ago when I was working with the State Department as a contractor in their antiterrorism program, and we brought foreign police officers to the country. When the wall came down in Eastern Europe with the demise of the Soviet Union, we began training police officers from Poland, Hungary, and then later Czechoslovakia. I especially remember a group of Polish police officers. We brought them to the States and took them to an Albertson's grocery store. I'll never forget the men walking in. They just froze. And some of them began to literally weep.

They didn't speak English, so I had to work through an interpreter, but the bottom line was they had never seen so much. They had become accustomed to standing in line, sometimes for hours, just to get whatever meager stock was in the store. Maybe a loaf of bread, maybe some milk. But they had never seen such abundance in all their lives, and they were overwhelmed by it.

You see, sometimes we live not realizing the abundance that exists in Christ Jesus. Paul asked God to answer his prayers for the Ephesians according to the riches of His glory, which are infinite. He prayed for their spiritual strength. Through the Spirit, he prayed that Jesus would be completely at home in their hearts, by faith—not just casually walking with Jesus, but they would live in such a way that they would be holy vessels rooted and grounded in love.

Paul wrote a lot about love. We only have one English word for *love*, but the Greek has several words for love. One is *agape* love, which is a benevolent, self-sacrificing love for others. It's not sexual love. And we should be rooted and grounded in *agape* love—sacrificing to benefit others. We've read this a lot in Paul's writings; what we do, especially in using our Christian liberty, should be to edify and encourage others, to build them up. We should do all things in love.

Then he prayed for us all to know the expanse of Christ's love for us, which passes knowledge. Paul said we can't even understand it. It surpasses our knowledge and our ability to comprehend. We can only experience it.

Pastor Adrian Rogers told a story[1] about a group of Napoleon's soldiers who made an impactful discovery in a Spanish dungeon after the Inquisition. They found a skeleton chained to one wall, and on the opposite wall they saw a cross the prisoner had apparently etched into the stone. At the apex of the cross, he had carved the word *height*. At the foot of the cross was the word *depth*. And on either side of the cross were the words *breadth* and *length*. To this prisoner, the cross gives us the dimensions of God's love that Paul prayed about here in Ephesians 3:17–19. The apostle prayed we would grow in our experience of the incredible love of Christ that was fully, finally, and forever expressed on the cross. Then Paul concluded by praying we should be filled with the fullness of God, a God who loves us so much that He was willing to give up His only Son (see Rom. 8:32).

In these first three chapters, we have studied the doctrinal section of Ephesians. Paul explained the foundation of the church and specifically the revelation of God's plan, the revelation of God's grace, and the revelation of the mystery. In chapter 4, we begin the practical section; we learn about Paul's explanation of how to function as the church in this world.

Questions for Reflection and Discussion

1. What is the mystery of Christ that has been revealed (see 3:1–6)?

2. What did Paul pray that we would grasp (see vv. 14–19)?
   a. Comprehend the dimensions of being in the faith
   b. Know the love of Christ that surpasses knowledge
   c. Be filled with the fullness of God
   d. All the above

Notes on Today's Bible Reading

— Day 5 —

Ephesians 4

Verse of the Day

> [A]nd be renewed in the spirit of your mind.
>
> — *Ephesians 4:23*

Please read the entire Scripture selection in your own Bible and highlight or underline verses that stand out to you before you read the observations and engage the questions below.

In chapter 4, we begin the practical section of Ephesians. Here Paul explained the function of the church, which is to walk worthy of the call. Our key verse is Ephesians 4:23, which says, "and be renewed in the spirit of your mind."

As a reminder, Paul wrote this letter along with three other epistles from prison. He was a prisoner in Rome between AD 62 and 64. The first half of Ephesians deals with the doctrine or the foundation of the church, and the second half deals with the function of the church. I'm not alone in this opinion, but Ephesians is one of if not the most significant letter Paul wrote.

Ephesus was a lost, heathen city. It was the home of the great temple to Diana, the fertility goddess, and prostitutes plied their trade from that temple, so the temptation to sexual sin was intense.

That was the backdrop to this immoral city. It was a center of Greek culture, but people came there from all over the Roman world. In Asia Minor, Ephesus was where Asia and Europe came together because it was on a major trade route. It was a commercial center, and with it came the temptation for greed and many other sins.

Ephesus was packed with people who needed the gospel of Jesus Christ. It was such a strategic city that Paul spent three years there, which was longer than he spent in any other place. But all of this was the backdrop to the teaching he provided for the Christians there. It was quite a similar culture to what we find ourselves in today, with all its temptations and challenges, so this book is especially relevant to us.

Paul began the second half of this letter with a call to walk with a renewed mind. Once asked on a radio program what was the biggest lesson he had ever learned, Dale Carnegie quickly replied, "By far the most vital lesson I have ever learned is the importance of what we think. If I knew what you think, I would know what you are. Our thoughts make us what we are."[2] Actually, what he was saying is built on biblical truth. Proverbs 23:7 says, "For as he thinks in his heart, so is he." So it's appropriate Paul began this first discussion on the practical application of the Christian faith with a focus on the mind.

As you might recall from chapter 3, the mystery was the fact God was saving both Gentiles and Jews by grace, through faith into the same body. Paul punctuated this theme of unity in 4:1–16. First, he called for maintaining unity through the virtues of humility, gentleness, long-suffering, and love. Then he declared the basis for that unity: They are one body unified by one Spirit, they have one Lord with one faith and one baptism, and they believe in one God. That is the definition of unity!

Yet Paul made it clear that unity does not mean uniformity. In fact, he went on to explain how the Spirit has given members of the body different grace gifts for various roles within the church with a goal of (1) equipping the saints for the work of ministry, (2) edifying the body of Christ, (3) unifying everyone in the faith, and (4) maturing them in Christ as the head of a redeemed humanity. It is this redeemed humanity that he explained further in this chapter and on into chapter 5.

Then Paul picked back up the focus on the mind in 4:17. He said don't be futile in our mind. The futile mind is characterized by wasteful, useless, and empty-headed depravity. Don't pursue useless things. Why would someone walk in futility? Well, it is the darkened understanding. They're spiritually blind. Their understanding is being alienated from the life of God because of ignorance brought about because of the willful blindness of their hearts.

The unregenerated person cannot see. How else do you explain politicians, including presidents, who are so devoted to abortion they refuse to support a law that would require an abortionist to aid a child born alive after a botched abortion? How else do you explain the transgender craze, where you are told you can determine your own gender? Yet Jesus, quoting Genesis, unequivocally declares there are only two (see Gen. 1:27; Matt. 19:4). So who's right?

The world's information is doubling every two years. I have more information in my phone than most people had access to in their entire lives a few decades ago. But even though we have all this information, we lack wisdom and understanding. Proverbs 9:10 says, "The fear of the Lord is the beginning of wisdom, and the knowledge of the Holy One is understanding." Romans 1:22 says, "Professing to be wise, they became fools." So there's this futile mind, and a darkened understanding causes it.

But then you must ask the question, How did their understanding become darkened? How did they get into that situation? Well, they were alienated from the life of God. There is a warning here of the progression that takes place. Immorality is always on the march. Sin never stands still. And Paul warned believers of the path of the Gentiles, those who deny God, that this is the path away from Him. See, they were alienated from the life of God because of willful ignorance. They were without excuse.

Romans 2:14–15 goes further, saying, "for when Gentiles, who do not have the law, by nature do the things in the law, these, although not having the law, are a law to themselves, who show the work of the law written in their hearts, their conscience also bearing witness, and between themselves their thoughts accusing or else excusing them." But how do we get to a point of a hardened heart? What does that look like? Well, it's a seared conscience. It's given over to immorality, so this is the futile mind—the mind Paul said to put off, and he said to renew our mind. Get a new mind.

How is the mind renewed? Not by absorbing media headlines or thinking the way the world does, but by coming to Christ and submitting to His Word (Rom. 12:2; Eph. 4:17–23). If we find ourselves comfortable with the "majority" view and indifferent to scriptural truth, we have a darkened understanding, and Scripture urges us to ask whether we truly know Jesus. To know Him is to have our minds enlightened (2 Cor. 4:6). We "hear" Jesus as faith rises from hearing the Word of God (Rom. 10:17; John 10:27).

That's why we're doing this personal study. People ask, "You're a public-policy organization in Washington—why encourage people to read the Bible?" Because understanding comes when truth remakes the heart; then we begin to see reality as it is, not merely as headlines present it (John 8:31–32; Ps. 119:130). Let us learn "the truth . . . in Jesus" and be renewed in the spirit of our minds (Eph. 4:21, 23).

A renewed mind is the key to a transformed life. The mind is so important, and to have a renewed mind, we must put off the old mind. Stop living as those who do not know Jesus and take action. If we don't change the way we think, if we don't put off our old ways, we'll just continue down this path.

Colossians 3:1–2 says, "If then you were raised with Christ, seek those things which are above, where Christ is, sitting at the right hand of God. Set your mind on things above, not on things on the earth." In the spirit of your mind, choose to put the things of the past behind you. To do so, you must change the way you think and what you think about. This is not the power of positive thinking. It's not turning over a new leaf. It's transformation by the truth of God's Word. The old maxim goes: Sow a thought, reap an action; sow an action, reap a habit; sow a habit, reap a character; sow a character, reap a destiny.

We've got to choose what we're going to fill our lives with, what we're going to fill our minds with. In Philippians 4:8–9, Paul wrote, "Finally, brethren, whatever things are true, whatever things are noble, whatever things are just, whatever things are pure, whatever things are lovely, whatever things are of good report, if there is any virtue and if there is anything praiseworthy—meditate on these things. The things which you learned and received and heard and saw in me, these do, and the God of peace will be with you."

So like changing out of old clothes and into new ones, Paul challenged every Christian to take off their old humanity and to put on their new humanity, in which the image of God is being restored in true righteousness and holiness (Eph. 4:20–24). Then for the balance of the chapter, he compared the old humanity with

God's intention for the new (vv. 25–32). Instead of lying, we are to speak truth. Instead of harboring anger, we should seek reconciliation. Instead of stealing, we should work so we can be generous. Instead of tearing down others, we are to build up others with our words. Instead of seeking revenge, we should forgive even as God in Christ forgave us. The old humanity grieves the Spirit, but the new humanity is transformed by the Spirit. This transformation takes time, but it is essential.

I remember forty years ago when I joined the Marine Corps as a teenage boy right out of high school. A week after I graduated, I was in boot camp in San Diego. They cut off my hair. Then they gave me uniforms. Oddly, they also handed me a paper bag. They told me to take all my civilian clothes and put them in that paper bag and put on the uniform of a Marine. The transformation was not immediate. It took a few months to become a Marine. But the transformation was so total, so complete, when I got off a plane to come home for leave after boot camp, my mom walked right by me and didn't recognize me.

When we put off the old and put on the new, it's not immediate. It is a process, but the first step to a transformed life is a renewed mind. And the way to have a renewed mind—not darkened and walking in the futile paths of the blind—is to know Jesus Christ. And I trust that you do know Him, but if you don't, I encourage you to reach out and simply ask the Lord to forgive you of your sins and by faith receive the grace He has given to us through His Son, Jesus Christ, in His death on the cross.

Questions for Reflection and Discussion

1. Who did the Lord give to equip the saints for the work of ministry (see vv. 11–12)?

2. How are we to respond to one another (see v. 32)?
    a. Be kind.
    b. Be tenderhearted.
    c. Be forgiving.
    d. All the above.

Notes on Today's Bible Reading

— Day 6 —
Ephesians 5

Verse of the Day

> For you were once darkness, but now you are light in the Lord. Walk as children of light.
>
> — *Ephesians 5:8*

Please read the entire Scripture selection in your own Bible and highlight or underline verses that stand out to you before you read the observations and engage the questions below.

In today's study, we are looking at chapter 5. Again, in this second half of the book of Ephesians, Paul covered the function of the church. Our key verse is Ephesians 5:8, which says, "For you were once darkness, but now you are light in the Lord. Walk as children of light." Having laid out the doctrine, the foundation of the church, in the first three chapters of Ephesians, Paul systematically instructed believers on the function of the church, meaning how they should live as followers of Jesus in a society that was in every way corrupted—morally, spiritually, politically, and culturally.

We read in chapter 4 that, for us as well, there must be a break with the past, a change of mind, a change of clothing per se—put off the old humanity; put on the new humanity. And in chapter 5, we are talking about what that new humanity looks like. How does a new person in Christ conduct himself or herself? That's what we're looking at in verses 1–13.

This chapter begins with the word *Therefore*, which means it is a continuation of Paul's previous discussion of breaking with the past and no longer walking in the futility of the mind as the world does. But how do we do that? Paul told the Ephesians at the very beginning of verse 1: "Be imitators of God," or better yet, Jesus. I think the message Paul conveyed in terms of the function of the church is we are *of* the light, we are *for* the light, and we should *be* light. So we come from God where we're the product of Jesus Christ. We should therefore live for God, for the light. And as a result, we should be light in the world.

Look at verse 8 again: "For you were once darkness, but now you are light in the Lord. Walk as children of light." See, we are the light; we are of the light. In John 8:12 Jesus said, "I am the light of the world. He who follows Me shall not walk in darkness, but have the light of life." So we are of the light, but we are also to be living for the light.

In Matthew 5:14 Jesus said, "You are the light of the world. A city that is set on a hill cannot be hidden." You see, we expose the darkness not necessarily with our words but through our lives, by the way we conduct ourselves. Look what Paul said in Ephesians 5:7–11: "Therefore do not be partakers with them. For you were once darkness, but now you are light in the Lord. Walk as children of light (for the fruit of the Spirit is in all goodness, righteousness, and truth), finding out what is acceptable to the Lord. And have no fellowship with the unfruitful works of darkness, but rather expose them." And we expose them by the way we live according to the truth, regardless of what the culture says.

Where old things have passed away, we put off the old self, and we put on the new spiritual self. And how do we do this? We become imitators of Christ. We are of the light when we are born again, when we accept Jesus Christ as our Lord and Savior. He says, "Look, I'm the Light of the world, and when you accept me, you are a part of the light." We have been bought with a price. So we're to live for the light, we're to walk as children of the light, and as a result, we become light to the world around us.

Then look at verses 14–16: "Therefore He says: 'Awake, you who sleep, arise from the dead, and Christ will give you light.' See then that you walk circumspectly, not as fools but as wise, redeeming the time, because the days are evil." Now, I find Paul's encouragement fascinating: "redeeming the time." It's almost like a transaction, an investment. Getting a return. Making the most of the time.

We often read the verse about how the days are evil, and we think of all the things happening now. Yes, these are certainly evil times; I don't dispute that. But that's not really what it's saying. Life is filled with challenges, with obstacles, in this fallen world, and those are going to come. But there are going to be times when we have an opportunity to make the most of the moment, to redeem the time. Maybe it's to share the gospel with someone. Maybe it's to take on a missionary project. It really can be anything the Lord is leading us to do. The next verse tells us how to do that. Look at Ephesians 5:17: "Therefore do not be unwise, but understand what the will of the Lord is." And how do we do this? How do we know what the will of God is? Again, we must be in the Word of God.

Look at verse 18: "And do not be drunk with wine, in which is dissipation; but be filled with the Spirit." So why is this mention of alcohol suddenly in the middle of this? That's not really what he's talking about. He's telling us not to waste our time. "Be wise, be filled with the Spirit." How do people become drunk? Well, they drink alcohol, and they are active participants. How are we filled with the Holy Spirit? We must be filling ourselves with the things of the Spirit. Paul said we're sealed by the Holy Spirit. When we're saved, we receive the Holy Spirit; we're sealed in the day of redemption. That's what I believe the Scripture says. But the degree to which we're filled with the Holy Spirit—influenced by, led by—is determined by how we yield ourselves to and fill our lives with the Holy Spirit through the reading of the Word, through prayer, through the "speaking to one another in psalms and hymns and spiritual songs, singing and making melody in your heart to the Lord" (v. 19).

Then verse 20 says, "giving thanks always for all things to God the Father in the name of our Lord Jesus Christ." Thanksgiving is really at the heart of this new life. Remember, Paul wrote from prison, "in everything give thanks; for this is the will of God in Christ Jesus for you" (1 Thess. 5:18). A key part of this is putting off the old self, putting on the new self, and having a heart of gratitude. It is powerful when we walk in gratitude and thanksgiving to the Lord, and this helps us redeem the time. Because if we're not thankful, we become angry, we're bitter because of the evil days, because of the difficult things we face. But when we are praying and we're thankful, even for the evil days, we are then understanding the will of God.

In Ephesians 5:21, Paul introduced this idea of "submitting to one another in the fear of God." Here he's talking about an attitude of giving and cooperating, assuming responsibility, and carrying a burden. Then Paul brought up a subject that has created controversy when he said in verse 22, "Wives, submit to your own husbands as to the Lord." The word *submit* can be used in a military connotation, which is an order like "get in line" or "close ranks," or it can be used in a more informal way like "follow me." Paul was asking wives to submit in this way. So first off, instead of having to submit to everyone, wives were under the covering of their husbands: "submit to your own husbands, as to the Lord. For the husband is head of the wife, as also Christ is head of the church; and He is the Savior of the body."

Then there is the word to the husbands in verse 25: "Husbands, love your wives, just as Christ also loved the church and gave Himself for her." Look at this in the context of the way Jesus operates. If a husband is to operate as Jesus did, Jesus said to those whom He invited to become His disciples, "deny himself, and take up his cross daily, and follow Me" (Luke 9:23). I can tell you right now the nature of God is not to demand that anyone follows Him. Jesus doesn't demand that we follow Him. He invites us to follow Him, then we submit to His leadership because we're following Him. That's what it's describing here. It's not ordering military structure, which I'll have to be honest, I didn't really get when I was first married.

In our early years, my wife and I struggled—mostly because I was still in the Marine Corps and tried to run our home like a platoon. I was wrong. When Ephesians 5 finally sank in, it reshaped my view of marriage. I saw that my calling was to love my wife as Christ loves the church—self-giving and sacrificial, laying down privileges. Jesus left the riches of heaven to redeem and sanctify His bride; that became my pattern. Through that lens I realized the problem in our marriage wasn't her—it was me, and I needed to change.

As husbands begin to lead sacrificially and wives submit to that loving leadership, it works beautifully. This is why it's crucial that husbands and wives have a relationship with Jesus Christ because that's the center. Without this transformative relationship of following Christ, it doesn't work. I know you can make it work, but it's difficult. My wife and I have been married for thirty-six years, and it's wonderful. It gets better every day because both of us are submitted to Christ and following in that way.

When we accept Jesus Christ as our Lord and Savior, we are filled with the Spirit, and under His controlling influence, we're able to submit to one another in the body. We are able to function lovingly in marriage and seize opportunities where we recognize we are of the light, we live for the light, and as a result, we are light to the world around us. So today, let's live as light!

Questions for Reflection and Discussion

1. Based on the analogy Paul gave, what does it mean to be "filled with the Spirit" (see v. 18)?

2. How is the marital relationship like the relationship between Christ and His church (vv. 25–32)?
   a. Wives are to submit to their husbands like the church to the Lord.
   b. Husbands are to love their wives like Christ loved the church and gave Himself sacrificially for her.
   c. Both of the above
   d. Neither of the above

Notes on Today's Bible Reading

— Day 7 —
Ephesians 6

Verse of the Day

> Therefore take up the whole armor of God, that you may be able to withstand in the evil day, and having done all, to stand.
>
> —*Ephesians 6:13*

Please read the entire Scripture selection in your own Bible and highlight or underline verses that stand out to you before you read the observations and engage the questions below.

Ephesians 6 is one of my favorite chapters in all the Scriptures. If you tune into "Washington Watch," you will recall that I sign off every day with Ephesians 6:13, my life verse and our key verse for today's study: "Therefore take up the whole armor of God, that you may be able to withstand in the evil day, and having done all, to stand."

In our previous study, we saw how Paul spoke of the transforming power of God's Spirit (5:18), whose controlling influence should permeate every area of life. This includes our devotional relationship with God in worship and thanksgiving (5:19–20), our respectful relationships with fellow church members (5:21), and our marital relationship (5:22–33).

The emphasis on the Spirit's influence continues in chapter 6 with our family relationships between parents and children and a special word to fathers (6:1–4). Paul included in this section a word about workplace relationships between servant and master, or as we think today, between employee and employer (6:5–9). Finally, Paul concluded the letter with the call to stand firm in the spiritual battle raging all around us, armed with God's strength, clothed with His armor, and persevering in prayer (6:10–20).

Let's dive in and look at 6:1–4. Speaking of the parent-child relationship, notice Paul instructed children first to obey then honor (vv. 1–3). There may be occasions when obedience is not possible, but honor is unconditional, and God will bless that honor. Pay close attention to this next verse, which is also a command: "Fathers, do not provoke your children to wrath" (v. 4a). That's the negative side of a father's potential influence.

I saw this headline recently: "Our greatest public health crisis? The angry young American male."[3] Others have pointed to the increase in mass shootings perpetrated by angry young men. Why might they be angry? The anger can often be traced to a rejection from their fathers, who were either never present in their lives, walked out, or were emotionally absent. The notion promoted that fathers are not essential to children is another one of those lies from the pit of hell. A father's presence and positive influence are absolutely critical to the success of children.

In fact, this brings us to the positive part of Paul's command to fathers regarding their children: "but bring them up in the training and admonition of the Lord" (v. 4b). It is imperative that fathers fulfill their biblical role to instruct, to encourage, and most importantly, to be an example to their children. This is one of the reasons the Family Research Council launched our Stand Courageous men's conferences a few years ago. We realized if men would follow the Lord, serve Him, and lead their families to do the same, we could solve most of the social pathologies in our nation. Spiritually engaged fathers leading their families are the key.

The next relationship Paul spoke about in 6:5–9 is between servants and masters, which we apply today to the workplace. We are to do our work "as to the Lord." And I have found this to be quite freeing in the various environments I've been in throughout my career. I've worked for some tough people, and I've worked for some people who didn't appreciate what I did and didn't recognize it. But I realized that I work for the Lord, and He is my boss. Consequently, we should work just as it says here in Ephesians 6:6–8: "not with eyeservice, as men-pleasers, but as bondservants of Christ, doing the will of God from the heart, with goodwill doing service, as to the Lord, and not to men." Knowing this is the key. "Whatever good anyone does, he will receive the same from the Lord, whether he is a slave or free." When we begin to realize we work for God and He's the one who will bring the increase, bless us, and prosper us even though someone else may sign our check, that's freeing.

We conclude the book by reviewing the things Paul said we need to do: How we need to live as children of the light. How we need to walk circumspectly, not as fools but as wise children of the light, putting off the old self and putting on the new. And how the Holy Spirit should be the controlling influence in all our various relationships with God, in the church, at home, and in the workplace. Paul gave us instruction after instruction on God's design for Christian living, how we are to function as believers, which was totally counterculture then as it is now.

Of course, this all can seem overwhelming. How can we possibly live this way? Here it is: "Finally, my brethren, be strong in the Lord and in the power of His might" (v. 10). To live this way, we must be empowered. Our strength is found in the power of God's might. We must have His strength, His courage and boldness, or what Paul told us next will be of little use.

Consider verse 11: "Put on the whole armor of God, that you may be able to stand against the wiles of the devil." If we don't have a heart of courage, we don't have any need for battle gear. Then Paul lifted the curtain on the real enemy in verse 12: "For we do not wrestle against flesh and blood, but against principalities, against powers, against the rulers of the darkness of this age, against spiritual hosts of wickedness in the heavenly places." This one verse tells us all we need to know about what we are up against. We are *not* battling people—we are fighting against all of *hell*, against Satan and his demons. These terms Paul used are not redundant; these are levels or ranks of what we are battling against as we are in the kingdom of God going against the forces of darkness. There are demonic forces over nations and regions, cities and territories, and even some unsaved people.

How are we to deal with them? Paul told us in verse 13: "Therefore take up the whole armor of God, that you may be able to withstand in the evil day, and having done all, to stand." We are to put on the armor God has provided and boldly stand in the power of God's might through the Holy Spirit, refusing to surrender or relent. Then Paul lists the armor in verses 14–17: belt of truth, breastplate of righteousness, footgear of gospel peace, shield of faith, helmet of salvation, and the sword of the Spirit—the Word of God. Unlike the other pieces of equipment designed to protect and defend, the sword, the Word of God, is designed to take ground and go on the offensive. And notice there's no armor for our backside, meaning no retreat.

Paul went on to describe the often forgotten but one of the most powerful weapons in our arsenal: "praying always with all prayer and supplication in the Spirit, being watchful to this end with all perseverance and supplication for all the saints" (v. 18). Look at the characteristics of this prayer: (1) praying always; remember, Paul said, "Pray without ceasing" (1 Thess. 5:17) and (2) persevering in prayer; Jesus told the parable of the widow and the politician to make the point that "men always ought to pray and not lose heart" (Luke 18:1). What are we to pray for? Everything! But especially pray for strength for ourselves and others. Look at what Paul asked for in Ephesians 6:19–20: "that utterance may be given to me, that I may open my mouth boldly to make known the mystery of the gospel, for which I am an ambassador in chains; that in it I may speak boldly, as I ought to speak."

This is incredible. Paul was already bold, but he is asking for even more boldness. Why was Paul in prison? For speaking boldly! Now he is asking for prayer so that he will continue to speak boldly. When I think of Paul, I don't think of timid, weak, or afraid. Yet I think Paul is being transparent in his request for boldness. There are times when we all get weary in the battle, and frankly, we want to step back, sit down, and go silent. We can't—too much is at stake! We need to pray for our leaders that they remain bold and courageous, inspiring others to do the same.

What a great chapter! Be strong in the Lord. The Christian life must be lived in the strength and the power of the Lord Jesus Christ. Be aware of what we are fighting against. It is not against flesh and blood. It is not a battle between Left and Right. It's not a battle between Republican and Democrat. It's not that complicated or confusing. In fact, it's really simple. It's a battle between good and evil. It's light against darkness. And how do we fight this spiritual battle? With spiritual weapons. Be prayed up, be equipped with the spiritual gear from God, be bold and committed to stand the ground God has entrusted to us.

Going back to my days in the Marine Corps and even in law enforcement, we had to have the right equipment. Our equipment not only protected us, but it also gave us the ability to perform the mission and the task we had been assigned. But all the weapons in the world are no substitute for courage and the strength that only comes from the Lord. Jesus said the devil's mission is to lie and steal, kill and destroy. Our mission is to follow the Lord Jesus Christ, take the fight to Satan, and take the light of Christ into the darkness that others might come to know Him and be set free from spiritual bondage. That challenge grows greater with each passing day. The way to turn the tide is to take our stand. Then, having prayed, prepared, and taken our stand, by all means, keep on standing!

Questions for Reflection and Discussion

1. What special parenting instructions are specifically given to fathers (see v. 4)?

2. What does the armor of God allow us to do (see vv. 11–14)?
   a. Take our stand against the devil's schemes
   b. When the day of evil comes, we may be able to stand our ground, and after having done everything, to stand.
   c. Stand firm
   d. All the above

Notes on Today's Bible Reading

— Day 8 —

Philippians 1

Verse of the Day

For to me, to live is Christ, and to die is gain.

— *Philippians 1:21*

Please read the entire Scripture selection in your own Bible and highlight or underline verses that stand out to you before you read the observations and engage the questions below.

Today, we begin Paul's letter to the Philippians. In Philippians 1, we find out how to live beyond fear. Our key verse is Philippians 1:21: "For to me, to live is Christ, and to die is gain." This letter is one of the four Paul wrote while he was under house arrest in Rome. Before we dig into our study of the text, let's consider the background and a brief overview of Philippians.

Background

The city of Philippi was named after Alexander the Great's father, Philip of Macedon. Later it became a Roman colony settled largely by army veterans. The city benefited greatly from the construction of the Via Egnatia, the major Roman road that connected the area to the Adriatic Sea in the south and the Dardanelles in the north. Philippi was a populous commercial center, and therefore a target-rich environment for the gospel.

Paul traveled to Philippi during his second missionary journey after the Spirit of God closed some doors, and it was interesting the way God called him to go there. In Acts 16:9–10, we read, "And a vision appeared to Paul in the night. A man of Macedonia stood and pleaded with him, saying, 'Come over to Macedonia and help us.' Now after he had seen the vision, immediately we sought to go to Macedonia, concluding that the Lord had called us to preach the gospel to them." So Paul went to the western part of Macedonia, where Philippi was located.

He first met with Lydia, a traveling business owner whom the Scripture records worshipped God but had not been saved and did not know about Jesus. She was converted to Christ through God opening her heart when she heard Paul's teaching. Silas was with Paul at the time. They were beaten and imprisoned because the Chamber of Commerce, basically, got mad when people turned from sin and demonic oppression, causing a decline in their business. Some things never change. And remember, while they were in prison, God sent an earthquake and the jailer was converted. That was the start of the church at Philippi, which was the first church Paul established in Europe.

Overview

We're going to see in this joy-filled letter that Paul had a lot of affection for the church in Philippi. And the members apparently had a strong feeling of connection to him as well because we know they sent at least two gifts of financial support to him, one of them while he was in prison in Rome. This letter is primarily Paul's response to their monetary support; it's really a "Thank You" note for sending the money to him while he was in prison. The letter divides itself generally along the lines of the four chapters: (1) Joy in Living for Jesus, (2) Joy in Serving Others Like Jesus, (3) Joy in Pursuing Only Jesus, and (4) Joy in Our Contentment in Jesus.

Commentary

Let's begin in Philippians 1:1: "Paul and Timothy, bondservants of Jesus Christ, To all the saints in Christ Jesus who are in Philippi, with the bishops and deacons." Notice how he included Timothy. I just think this is great. Here was Paul writing a letter, and it may be that Timothy wrote it for him as his scribe, but he included Timothy in this because he was Paul's son in the ministry. Paul was mentoring and raising up Timothy to take over responsibilities as a leader.

Continue with 1:2–5: "Grace to you and peace from God our Father and the Lord Jesus Christ. I thank my God upon every remembrancc of you, always in every prayer of mine making request for you all with joy, for your fellowship in the gospel from the first day until now." Obviously, Paul was a man of prayer, and he was thanking God for the Philippian believers. They were so special to him that he said every thought of them elicited thanksgiving to God. Of course, we're to be thankful, but these folks just held a special place in Paul's heart that every time he thought of them, he said, "Lord, I thank You for them." They were partners with Paul, and there was true fellowship, *koinonia*, community. They were a part of his life, a part of his ministry.

Next look at the key thought in 1:6: "being confident of this very thing, that He who has begun a good work in you will complete it until the day of Jesus Christ." What a promise! And I think this is how Paul, in part, was not only able to survive all that he went through but actually thrive in the difficulties he faced: He was confident that God would complete what He had begun. You see, our hope should not be built upon what we see today but on what we know that we will see someday by the power and the authority of the Word of God. What God has begun in our lives, He will bring to completion. Count on it!

Let's continue in Philippians 1:7: "just as it is right for me to think this of you all, because I have you in my heart, inasmuch as both in my chains and in the defense and confirmation of the gospel, you all are partakers with me of grace." Here again Paul alluded to their partnership with him. He was saying, "Look, all that I'm enduring, you're enduring. You're a part of this." Next consider Paul's passion and his prayer in 1:8–11: "For God is my witness, how greatly I long for you all with the affection of Jesus Christ. And this I pray, that your love may abound still more and more in knowledge and all discernment, that you may approve the things that are excellent, that you may be sincere and without offense till the day of Christ, being filled with the fruits of righteousness which are by Jesus Christ, to the glory and praise of God."

Paul then transitioned to the heart of the matter of this first chapter, which is where we're going to focus most of our time in this study. Here is the main takeaway: Paul's courage of conviction in following Jesus in the face of opposition inspired confidence in others to live boldly for Jesus without fear. Let's see how he built his case beginning in Philippians 1:12–13: "But I want you to know, brethren, that the things which happened to me have actually turned out for the furtherance of the gospel, so that it has become evident to the whole palace guard, and to all the rest, that my chains are in Christ." This letter was written from prison because Paul had been preaching the gospel. Consider the way Paul described the sacrifices he had made in ministry over in 2 Corinthians 11:23–28:

> Are they ministers of Christ?—I speak as a fool—I am more: in labors more abundant, in stripes above measure, in prisons more frequently, in deaths often. From the Jews five times I received forty stripes minus one. Three times I was beaten with rods; once I was stoned; three times I was shipwrecked; a night and a day I have been in the deep; in journeys often, in perils of waters, in perils of robbers, in perils of my own countrymen, in perils of the Gentiles, in perils in the city, in perils in the wilderness, in perils in the sea, in perils among false brethren; in weariness and toil, in sleeplessness often, in hunger and thirst, in fastings often, in cold and nakedness—besides the other things, what comes upon me daily: my deep concern for all the churches.

Wow! This guy had seen it all. Yet Paul had the courage of conviction to advance the gospel even though he was chained to a Roman guard!

What amazes me is Paul's providential perspective on his circumstances: "But I want you to know, brethren, that the things which happened to me have actually turned out for the furtherance of the gospel" (1:12). That is a living example of Romans 8:28: "And we know that all things work together for good to those who love God, to those who are the called according to His purpose." The good that he talked about is to glorify God and to advance His purposes and His kingdom. It only works out for our good when we are submitted to and in alignment with God's purposes. God is first.

It is all about Him. It's not about us. So, when we align ourselves with Him, the good—in terms of God being glorified in His kingdom—advances. We benefit from it when we're aligned with Him.

But there's more.

Notice in Philippians 1:14: "and most of the brethren in the Lord, having become confident by my chains, are much more bold to speak the word without fear." I have made this statement many times: "Courage breeds courage." When a person steps out with courage, it inspires others to do the same. We see this again and again in Scripture and indeed in our lives today. The chains of opposition met with the courage of our conviction in Jesus Christ will lead to the confidence in others to live for Jesus without fear. So how do we have this courage? How do we come to live beyond fear?

Let's go back to our key verse for today: "For to me, to live is Christ, and to die is gain" (v. 21). So how do we intimidate someone who has this outlook on life? I mean, really, how do we stop someone who has this outlook on life? Someone who says, "For me to live is Christ, to die is gain." The answer is we don't. This is how we live beyond fear. It is getting to the place where we declare, "I've been crucified with Christ. For me to live is Christ. To die is gain. I can't be canceled." That's what Paul was saying.

Then Paul looked at the implications of both options: "But if I live on in the flesh, this will mean fruit from my labor; yet what I shall choose I cannot tell. For I am hard-pressed between the two, having a desire to depart and be with Christ, which is far better. Nevertheless to remain in the flesh is more needful for you. And being confident of this, I know that I shall remain and continue with you all for your progress and joy of faith, that your rejoicing for me may be more abundant in Jesus Christ by my coming to you again" (Phil. 1:22–26). Obviously, death was the better option because he would instantly be with his beloved Jesus. Yet Paul was such an amazing servant of the Lord that he was willing to continue on in this life, even if it meant imprisonment, if for no other reason than to encourage them on their journey with Jesus. Yet by faith, he remained confident of his release and his continued ministry.

Now, there's one more aspect of this courage and confident living in the face of opposition. Paul pointed to the necessity of unity: "Only let your conduct be worthy of the gospel of Christ, so that whether I come and see you or am absent, I may hear of your affairs, that you stand fast in one spirit, with one mind striving together for the faith of the gospel, and not in any way terrified by your adversaries, which is to them a proof of perdition, but to you of salvation, and that from God" (Phil. 1:27–28). We are to be unified. And as we're unified, that gives us the strength. And quite honestly, that is intimidating to the other side, to the forces of darkness.

Let's finish with Philippians 1:29–30: "For to you it has been granted on behalf of Christ, not only to believe in Him, but also to suffer for His sake, having the same conflict which you saw in me and now hear is in me." The courage of your conviction in following Jesus in the face of opposition will inspire others to live boldly for Jesus Christ without fear of what others might say or do. Living like that, frankly, will turn the world upside down. This frightens the enemy of our souls, and that's why the enemy wants us to live in fear of man rather than of the Lord. Because when we live with no fear, we can serve the Lord faithfully and effectively.

What a powerful chapter! And I pray that we could all come to that point where we would say with Paul, "For me to live is Christ, to die is gain." That our lives would be about living for God, about knowing Him and making Him known. And if we die before Christ returns, that we have the certainty that we will be with Him forever and ever, which, as Paul said, is much better. Yet until then, we have work to do here; we need to be working to advance the kingdom, and thus bring glory to God. That is our purpose. There is joy in living for Jesus and fulfilling that purpose.

Unfortunately, many people wander through life without a sense of purpose, and they lack joy. I believe this is why we see the growth of suicides and drug addictions. People are looking for purpose and meaning because without it, life has no meaning. In fact, life is worthless and joyless. In God, however, we have purpose. There is joy in living for Christ. And I pray that if anyone in your circle of relationships is living a life without purpose, a life without joy, that you will encourage them to turn to Jesus. I pray they might open their hearts, that they might reach out and receive by faith the forgiveness found in Jesus Christ and be made whole, that their life might find purpose and meaning and joy, and that they too could say with Paul, "For me to live is Christ, to die is gain."

Questions for Reflection and Discussion

1. After reading this first chapter, what is the overall tone?
   a. Fretful
   b. Joyful
   c. Mournful
   d. None of the above

2. According to Paul, to live is Christ, but to die is what (see v. 21)?

Notes on Today's Bible Reading

— Day 9 —

Philippians 2

Verse of the Day

> Let this mind be in you which was also in Christ Jesus.
> — *Philippians 2:5*

Please read the entire Scripture selection in your own Bible and highlight or underline verses that stand out to you before you read the observations and engage the questions below.

Today we study Philippians 2. Before we begin, consider this question: Do you want the Lord to give you a piece of His mind? That's what we're going to look at today. Our key verse is Philippians 2:5, which says, "Let this mind be in you which was also in Christ Jesus." As we talked about before, Philippians is a thank-you letter from Paul to the believers at Philippi for the gift they sent to him to meet his financial needs while he was in prison in Rome. In chapter 1, we saw in Paul the joy that comes from living for Jesus despite his incarceration. Chapter 2 covers the joy that comes from serving others like Jesus. Based on the example of the Son of God, who left heaven and humbled Himself to die on a cross, Paul called for unity that can only come through that kind of selfless humility.

Let's start in Philippians 2:1: "Therefore if there is any consolation in Christ, if any comfort of love, if any fellowship of the Spirit, if any affection and mercy." Now let me just stop there for a moment. This "if" is not a question. Paul presented an argument. "If there is any consolation in Christ," and we know that there is; if any comfort of love, any fellowship of the Spirit, any affection and mercy," which there are, "then do this."

Let's continue in verse 2: "fulfill my joy by being like-minded, having the same love, being of one accord, of one mind." And it is because of this support, this help, this consolation of Christ, that we can actually be in unity. Then verse 3: "Let nothing be done through selfish ambition or conceit, but in lowliness of mind let each esteem others better than himself." Selfish ambition is a unity killer. So Paul basically said, "Rather than having selfish ambition, esteem others. Put others and their interests before you." Now that's easily said but difficult to do.

One time I was at a church in South Carolina, and the worship team was singing. I enjoyed the worship. It was great. But one of the lead singers' microphone went dead. He was playing the guitar, so his hands were busy and he couldn't fix the microphone. Well, one of the other lead singers went over and gave her microphone to him. As I watched, she kept singing without a microphone. This was esteeming someone else more highly than herself. She didn't stop singing. You know why? Because she was singing to the Lord. He doesn't need a PA system to hear us. We don't need the big platform for God to see us. We need to esteem others greater than ourselves. What an example!

Let's continue in Philippians 2:4, "Let each of you look out not only for his own interests, but also for the interests of others." But how can we accomplish such a difficult task? The answer is in verse 5: "Let this mind be in you which was also in Christ Jesus." Now, here it is: Have the mind of Christ. Follow His example. What follows is one of the most profound descriptions of Jesus in all the New Testament. Look at verses 6–8: "who, being in the form of God, did not consider it robbery to be equal with God, but made Himself of no reputation, taking the form of a bondservant, and coming in the likeness of men. And being found in appearance as a man, He humbled Himself and became obedient to the point of death, even the death of the cross." Jesus humbled Himself. It wasn't forced on Him. He humbled Himself to the point of the humiliating death on the cross. His humility paved the way for our salvation.

Yet because Jesus was willing to humble Himself to accomplish the plan and purposes of the Father, He was exalted. Look at Philippians 2:9–11: "Therefore God also has highly exalted Him and given Him the name which is above every name, that at the name of Jesus every knee should bow, of those in heaven, and of those on earth, and of those under the earth, and that every tongue should confess that Jesus Christ is Lord, to the glory of God the Father." Because Jesus humbled Himself before all, God is exalting Him above all. But don't miss the application because Jesus is our pattern for living a God-honoring life. James put it this way: "Humble yourselves in the sight of the Lord, and He will lift you up" (James 4:10). Have the mind of Christ, follow His example. It is the example of humble self-sacrifice borne out of love—love for the Father and love for us.

Moving on in Philippians 2: "Therefore, my beloved, as you have always obeyed, not as in my presence only, but now much more in my absence, work out your own salvation with fear and trembling; for it is God who works in you both to will and to do for His good pleasure" (vv. 12–13). What was Paul saying here? Do we work out our own salvation? Is that up to us? No. Through our obedience in the Lord, what was worked in us through the Holy Spirit by God's grace, is worked out, sanctifying us. We have a personal responsibility. Paul said, "You don't need me to be there to do this. You work this out with God who is working in you." And it's kind of like when we go to a gym and work out. We're going to build muscles, especially if we are lifting weights. We don't build muscles by sitting on the couch watching TV. Well, the same thing applies here. We don't build spiritual muscles by not engaging spiritually. We must read the Word, pray, seek the Lord, and obey what He tells us.

Now after this, Paul returned to the issue of humility and not operating or acting out of selfishness. Look at verse 14: "Do all things without complaining and disputing." (That was a favorite verse quoted around our house when the kids were little.) And here is what comes from humbling ourselves and not seeking our own to the destruction and division of others. Look at verse 15: "that you may become blameless and harmless, children of God without fault in the midst of a crooked and perverse generation, among whom you shine as lights in the world." When we're not putting ourselves first, when we're not creating strife and division, but we're walking in humility, and we have the mind of Christ, the result is that we become like our heavenly Father—our conduct in this fallen and evil world will shine like a light. It literally means like luminaries to the world, the sun and the moon, which provide comfort and direction. That's what we become in this dark world and even more so now as we live in a tumultuous time of uncertainty and difficulty. When we are living in obedience to God and there's unity in the body of Christ, it speaks volumes to a world that's looking for peace and direction.

Let's continue in Philippians 2:16: "holding fast the word of life, so that I may rejoice in the day of Christ that I have not run in vain or labored in vain." We're to hold onto the light of truth that has been given to us and hold it high. It's almost like a runner with a torch. We're to hold onto it because it gives strength and comfort to us. It gives direction to us. But to hold it forth, not only hold it fast, but hold it forth so that others can benefit from the light that we have been given in Christ Jesus.

In the remainder of the chapter, Paul offered commendations of trusted ministry team members who were serving others like Jesus. First, he commended the service of Timothy, his spiritual son. These were uplifting words of affirmation. I have to think that when Timothy read these or wrote them, if he wrote the letter for Paul, that it really spoke to him, fortified him. Look at verses 19–24:

> But I trust in the Lord Jesus to send Timothy to you shortly, that I also may be encouraged when I know your state. For I have no one like-minded, who will sincerely care for your state. For all seek their own, not the things which are of Christ Jesus. But you know his proven character, that as a son with his father he served with me in the gospel. Therefore I hope to send him at once, as soon as I see how it goes with me. But I trust in the Lord that I myself shall also come shortly.

I can only imagine how those words built up Timothy, encouraging him in a rather difficult calling.

Next we turn to Paul's commendation of Epaphroditus, whom scholars believe was a leader, perhaps a deacon at Philippi. Epaphroditus brought the gift from them to Paul, and in the course of the mission and the ministry that he was doing, he became sick, nearly dying as a result. Look at Philippians 2:25–28:

> Yet I considered it necessary to send to you Epaphroditus, my brother, fellow worker, and fellow soldier, but your messenger and the one who ministered to my need; since he was longing for you all, and was distressed because you had heard that he was sick. For indeed he was sick almost unto death; but God had mercy on him, and not only on him but on me also, lest I should have sorrow upon sorrow. Therefore I sent him the more eagerly, that when you see him again you may rejoice, and I may be less sorrowful.

So Epaphroditus took the letter from Paul and delivered it to the church. Let's continue in verses 29–30: "Receive him therefore in the Lord with all gladness, and hold such men in esteem; because for the work of Christ he came close to death, not regarding his life, to supply what was lacking in your service toward me." Epaphroditus served Paul and met his needs, just like Jesus.

There is joy in serving others like Christ did. When we live with the mind of Christ, esteeming others better than ourselves, not even death has a grip on us. Nor can fear overshadow us. As Paul said in Philippians 1:21, "For to me, to live is Christ, and to die is gain."

Questions for Reflection and Discussion

1. What does it mean to have the mind or attitude of Christ (see 2:5–11)?

2. How did Paul describe his "brother" Epaphroditus, who risked his life for the gospel (see vv. 25–30)?
    a. Fellow worker
    b. Fellow soldier
    c. Messenger
    d. Minister to Paul's need
    e. All of the above

Notes on Today's Bible Reading

— Day 10 —

Philippians 3

Verse of the Day

> I press on toward the goal for the prize of the upward call of God in Christ Jesus.
>
> — *Philippians 3:14*

Please read the entire Scripture selection in your own Bible and highlight or underline verses that stand out to you before you read the observations and engage the questions below.

As we study Philippians 3, here is the question: Are you living life in the rearview mirror? In this chapter, Paul basically answered, "I'm not looking back. I am pressing forward." In our key verse, Paul declared, "I press toward the goal for the prize of the upward call of God in Christ Jesus" (v. 14). The message is that there is joy in pursuing only Jesus. Remember, the letter to the Philippians is basically a "Thank You" letter to the believers at Philippi, but Paul took an opportunity to address a few problems along the way. We looked at one of these in the previous chapter, and that was a division in the church, a threat to the unity of the body.

As we read chapter 3, he returned to the threat posed by the deceptive teachings of the Judaizers. I say "returned" because unfortunately this is a common problem Paul encountered on the mission field and addressed in his letters. Now recall that Judaizers were mainly Jewish believers and their Gentile converts who held that the Levitical laws of the Old Testament were still binding, that believers were still under certain aspects of Mosaic Law, including circumcision.

Consequently, Paul spoke to this issue quite extensively in Galatians, which he wrote after the Council of Jerusalem around AD 48 or 49, in which this whole issue was the main topic. In Galatians 3:23–25, Paul explained that the law served a purpose: "But before faith came, we were kept under guard by the law, kept for the faith which would afterward be revealed. Therefore, the law was our tutor to bring us to Christ, that we might be justified by faith. But after faith has come, we are no longer under a tutor." In other words, we are not and cannot be saved by keeping the law—nor a combination of faith and law. It's not works or faith and works that gives us right standing before God. It is through faith alone in God's grace alone in Christ alone that we are made righteous before God.

Paul also warned the Philippian believers about this issue. He then inserted a parenthetical discussion of his own life example, that he was a "Hebrew of the Hebrews," but he didn't hang his hat on that for his salvation. He also warned his readers to avoid the examples of those who were teaching such a message that ran counter to the message of the cross. He urged instead, "Listen to what I'm teaching you and watch what I do. Follow my example. It's consistent with the gospel."

So the Word of God should remain the standard for the church. Everything we do and everything we hear, everything we get from pastors, preachers, teachers, everything we say should be measured according to the Word of God. That is the standard. But we need to know it. That's why we are on this journey through the Bible, so we can know the Word of God for ourselves and then examine all things in the light of the Word.

Let's take a closer look, beginning with Philippians 3:1–3: "Finally, my brethren, rejoice in the Lord. For me to write the same things to you is not tedious, but for you it is safe. Beware of dogs, beware of evil workers, beware of the mutilation! For we are the circumcision, who worship God in the Spirit, rejoice in Christ Jesus, and have no confidence in the flesh." Clearly, Paul had strong opinions about these Judaizers, calling them dogs, evil workers, and mutilators because of their insistence on physical circumcision in order to be in right standing with God. It is better instead to trust in the circumcision of the heart performed by the Spirit of God!

Now let's continue with Paul's line of argument with his own personal example in verses 4–7:

> . . . though I also might have confidence in the flesh. If anyone else thinks he may have confidence in the flesh, I more so: circumcised the eighth day, of the stock of Israel, *of* the tribe of Benjamin, a Hebrew of the Hebrews; concerning the law, a Pharisee; concerning zeal, persecuting the church; concerning the righteousness which is in the law, blameless. But what things were gain to me, these I have counted loss for Christ. Yet indeed I also count all things loss for the excellence of the knowledge of Christ Jesus my Lord, for whom I have suffered the loss of all things, and count them as rubbish, that I may gain Christ.

Saul of Tarsus was the prototypical Jew. His stature, His standing, all of those things that his fellow Jews would say, "Wow, he's the real deal. This man exceeds all his contemporaries as a model of the Mosaic Law and zeal for the Jewish faith." Yet he says, "I count that stuff as rubbish compared to what I have in Christ Jesus." Paul was saying, "Nothing that I strove for in strict adherence to my religion or tried to obtain in my own strength compares to what was freely given to me in Christ Jesus."

Then in 3:9–11, Paul pressed the case of justification before God by faith alone in Christ alone: "and be found in Him, not having my own righteousness, which is from the law, but that which is through faith in Christ, the righteousness which is from God by faith; that I may know Him and the power of His resurrection, and the fellowship of His sufferings, being conformed to His death, if, by any means, I may attain to the resurrection from the dead." Take note here that the Christian faith is not about adherence to a set of religious rules, but it is about a real relationship with Jesus Christ. It is not about following laws but following the living Lord! Basically Paul said, "More than anything else in life, I want to know Jesus and be like Jesus and draw my strength from Jesus!"

In the next few verses, Paul made clear that he is on a journey. He was on his way, pressing forward. He had not arrived. He had not yet been perfected. On numerous occasions, Paul said, "Follow my example," which I think he had the credibility to say. But even so, look at the way he framed this in verses 12–14: "Not that I have already attained, or am already perfected; but I press on, that I may lay hold of that for which Christ Jesus has also laid hold of me. Brethren, I do not count myself to have apprehended; but one thing I do, forgetting those things which are behind and reaching forward to those things which are ahead, I press toward the goal for the prize of the upward call of God in Christ Jesus."

Paul liked to use pictures and analogies in his writings, which is an effective means of communication because we think in pictures.

When someone tells you something, you're creating an image in your mind. So Paul described the Christian life as if it were a race. When in a race, the runners don't look back. They look forward. Why? Well, looking backward, they are prone to stumble.

Looking back can take several forms in our lives. Peter was a notable example of this in his failed attempt to walk on water. When Jesus approached the boat in the midst of a storm, Peter tried to walk out to Jesus, but he took his eyes off Jesus and looked back at the waves. We all know what happened, right? Peter began to sink. Let's be candid. We all do what Peter did. In fact, there have been times when I find myself in the midst of a challenge, and I am tempted to look back to less stressful times or maybe when I felt I was more productive or more impactful. But while we can learn from the past, we're not to live in the past. We should not look back lest we stumble and sink from the position God has placed us in today.

Now, there's another way that we look back. And I think Paul may have been tempted to do this. When he spoke of his zeal in persecuting the church before he came to Christ, I have to think there were times when Paul thought about the Christians he persecuted, those he arrested and threw into jail and others he condemned to death. It may have haunted him even after he repented, came to Christ, and became the greatest advocate for believers of his age. Yet Paul declared that he was "forgetting those things which are behind," things in the past. I think Paul pressed forward. Why? Because his past was under the blood of Jesus. We too can press forward without the baggage of our past. The Scripture says, "If we confess our sins, [God] is faithful and just to forgive us our sins and to cleanse us from all unrighteousness" (1 John 1:9). Let's not look back.

Maybe you are reading this, and the sins of your past haunt you. Satan, who is the accuser, will often bring up your past in order to cause you to stumble in your faith, stumble in the mission that God has called you to, and tell you that you are "unworthy." Yet Paul said, "What's behind is behind. I'm looking forward." And so don't look behind to past mistakes. Learn from them, but don't look back to choices you made that were not perfect and not the best. If you've confessed them before God, move forward and pursue the high calling of God in Christ Jesus. After we come to Christ, we still make mistakes. We must confess our sins, repent of them, and trust the Lord to forgive us, and He will! We can be free of our past. It should no longer control us nor define us.

As we wrap up our study, let's look at Philippians 3:15–17: "Therefore let us, as many as are mature, have this mind; and if in anything you think otherwise, God will reveal even this to you. Nevertheless, to the degree that we have already attained, let us walk by the same rule, let us be of the same mind. Brethren, join in following my example, and note those who so walk, as you have us for a pattern." Basically, he said, "Watch me and others like me who are walking with the Lord. You have us as an example."

So in this chapter, Paul said, "I'm not looking back, but I'm looking forward lest I stumble in this race we call life." Our lives are stained with sin. They're marked with mistakes. But once we have repented, our past is covered under the blood, and we are not to look back. We are to press on to better things ahead: The prize of the upward call of God in Christ Jesus. There is joy in pursuing Jesus!

Questions for Reflection and Discussion

1. After Paul took us on a journey through his "trophy case" of personal attributes and accomplishments, compared to his relationship with Christ, what did he call it all (see vv. 1–8)?

2. What is the goal we should press toward that Paul sums up as the "upward call of God in Christ Jesus" (see vv. 10–14)?
   a. To know Jesus
   b. To experience the power of His resurrection
   c. To become more like Jesus, even to the point of suffering and death
   d. All of the above

Notes on Today's Bible Reading

— Day 11 —
Philippians 4

Verse of the Day

> Therefore, my beloved and longed-for brethren, my joy and crown, so stand fast in the Lord, beloved.
>
> — *Philippians 4:1*

Please read the entire Scripture selection in your own Bible and highlight or underline verses that stand out to you before you read the observations and engage the questions below.

As we wrap up our study of Philippians, we are going to dive into what I consider to be the crescendo to this short letter that Paul wrote to the Philippians, as we look at the closing chapter, which is filled with familiar verses. In fact, *Christian Post* reported that the most marked verse on the Bible App in 2024 was Philippians 4:6: "Be anxious for nothing, but in everything by prayer and supplication, with thanksgiving, let your requests be made known to God."[4] There are others in this chapter, like verse 13, which is a favorite of athletes: "I can do all things through Christ who strengthens me." Yet seeing these popular verses in their context makes them even more powerful.

For those who are looking for peace and joy, look no further. Here it is. Our key verse is Philippians 4:1, "Therefore, my beloved and longed-for brethren, my joy and crown, so stand fast in the Lord, beloved." Here's a spoiler alert. I'm going to give the answer to the question, How do we find contentment, peace, and joy in this world? We just read it. "Stand fast in the Lord." Persevering in the Lord is the key, and Paul addressed three areas of standing firm in Christ in this chapter that lead to sustaining peace and joy.

First, stand fast in unity. Look at verses 1–4: "Therefore, my beloved and longed-for brethren, my joy and crown, so stand fast in the Lord, beloved. I implore Euodia and I implore Syntyche to be of the same mind in the Lord. And I urge you also, true companion, help these women who labored with me in the gospel, with Clement also, and the rest of my fellow workers, whose names are in the Book of Life. Rejoice in the Lord always. Again I will say, rejoice!"

There was a conflict between two prominent women in the Philippian church who "labored with [Paul] in the gospel." They helped him get the church started. And this is probably what prompted Paul in the first part of this letter to talk about standing firm in one spirit, with one mind, striving together for the faith of the gospel. "I implore Euodia and Syntyche to be of the same mind in the Lord" (v. 2). He even asked the others in the church to help these women to come together. You see, we need unity in the body of Christ, both the local church and in general between believers. Now, that doesn't mean we all wear the same uniforms or that we all act the same and look the same and talk the same. But there should be a core unity.

Remember, one of the illustrations Paul used of the church is that of a body: many members, but one body. This is so important. We need unity in the body. This, along with holiness, is one of the greatest needs in the body of Christ today. And I'll be the first to admit that I struggle with this. So please pray for me. Pray that I can pursue unity because it's more easily said than done, and it can only be accomplished, as Paul wrote earlier in this book, when we have the mind of Christ. That is the foundation for it. And when we have this unity, we can do what he says here: "Rejoice in the Lord always. Again, I will say, rejoice!"

Next, stand firm in prayer and thanksgiving. Look at Philippians 4:5–6: "Let your gentleness be known to all men. The Lord is at hand. Be anxious for nothing, but in everything by prayer and supplication, with thanksgiving, let your requests be made known to God." The antidote to anxiety is prayer. So don't worry, pray. Give it to God. And do it with gratitude because you know He will answer. I like the comment offered by Dr. Henry Halley: "Gratitude to God for what He does give us will surely incline Him to grant that which we do not have."[5] Thanksgiving really tills the soil of our heart so God can plant more.

Let's continue in verse 7: "and the peace of God, which surpasses all understanding, will guard your hearts and minds through Christ Jesus." Wow, that is powerful! So how can we do that in this world in which we live, where things are so challenging? I mean, it appears that the world is spinning out of control. We have ungodly leaders zealously pushing everything that is contrary to the truth of God. So how do we have peace and joy in this world? Look at verses 8–9: "Finally, brethren, whatever things are true, whatever things are noble, whatever things are just, whatever things are pure, whatever things are lovely, whatever things are of good report, if there is any virtue and if there is anything praiseworthy—meditate on these things. The things which you learned and received and heard and saw in me, these do, and the God of peace will be with you."

Consequently, here are some questions to consider: What are you watching? What are you listening to? What are you meditating upon? If you're watching cable news and listening to talk radio

24/7, I would encourage you to tune into "Washington Watch." We approach the news from a biblical perspective. We cannot ignore what is happening around us. But at the same time, we don't want to be inundated with the negative news from a humanist worldview that leaves us hopeless because man is helpless. What we need to do is look at these things through the lens of Scripture.

Now, we're not to bury our heads in the sand and ignore what is going on. That is just as wrong. I mean, look back at Philippians 4:6. We need to be praying through the challenges in our lives and in our world. And I believe that prayer moves the hand of God and it changes the hearts of men, including our own. As we pray, we're reminded that God is the Creator and the Sustainer of all that is, and we're not left in this world to fend for ourselves. We have access to the King of kings and the Lord of lords.

Look at verse 10: "But I rejoiced in the Lord greatly that now at last your care for me has flourished again; though you surely did care, but you lacked opportunity." I want to pause here and focus just on this verse for a moment because there's a great spiritual truth I do not want us to miss. Paul, more than wanting their gift for his own benefit (in chap. 2, he acknowledged his need, I believe), basically said, "I want you to have the reward that comes from sharing in this work." I think this is a great guide for giving when it comes to our resources and what we sow into ministries, into God's kingdom. We want to look at the ministry or the organization to which we are giving our resources as stewards of what God has entrusted to us, advancing the kingdom of God.

Kingdom work isn't always obvious. Family Research Council is often labeled as a "political" organization, but the better question to ask of us or any organization is this: Does it advance the kingdom of God? Look at the fruit. Look at our ministry to men and women in public leadership, our Stand on the Word emphasis, and equipping believers to live their faith in every sphere. When pastors tell me, "I just want to preach the gospel," I answer: "So do we—which is why we labor to align public policy with biblical truth, so the gospel can be preached freely and lived openly." We contend for religious liberty and human dignity so Christians can follow Christ at work, in schools, and on campus. It's like Paul: his imprisonment didn't look like progress, yet his chains advanced the gospel (Phil. 1:12–14), and the church partnered with him in support (Phil. 4:15–16). So we must be Spirit-led and discerning, investing in what endures—laying up treasures in heaven (Matt. 6:20).

Now we move to the final point. Stand firm in Christ. Look at Philippians 4:11–12: "Not that I speak in regard to need, for I have learned in whatever state I am, to be content: I know how to be abased, and I know how to abound. Everywhere and in all things I have learned both to be full and to be hungry, both to abound and to suffer need." There is joy in finding our contentment in Jesus.

Then we come to another famous verse: "I can do all things through Christ who strengthens me" (v. 13). This passage has also been taken out of context and used as a sort of "Superman" verse. Again, it is the favorite of athletes, but look at it in the context of this passage and it is even more powerful. I can have peace and joy in every situation that I may encounter in life, both good and bad. How can you have that peace and joy? Through Christ Jesus who strengthens us. Are you looking for peace and joy? Stand firm in unity. Stand firm in prayer and thanksgiving. And stand firm in the Lord Jesus Christ.

Let's close with Philippians 4:19–23 and yet another popular verse: "And my God shall supply all your need according to His riches in glory by Christ Jesus. Now to our God and Father be glory forever and ever. Amen. Greet every saint in Christ Jesus. The brethren who are with me greet you. All the saints greet you, but especially those who are of Caesar's household. The grace of our Lord Jesus Christ be with you all. Amen." Verse 19 is yet another one that many misread. The "name it and claim it" crowd needs to check the fine print on this one. Paul said God will supply all our *need*, not our *greed*. Some get confused at that point and think God is like an unlimited ATM. Yet when we have a legitimate need, humbly place it before our Father, and if it is in alignment with His will, He will open the storehouses of heaven and meet that need through Jesus. That's why all glory goes to God.

As we conclude our study of Philippians, if peace and joy are absent in your life, I pray for you. With all the things we're facing in this world—the spiritual warfare raging around us and the battles we must engage in every day—it is all too easy to lose our peace and our joy. This is especially true if we take our eyes off of Christ. But I pray we will stand firm in Him. That we will stand firm in unity. That we will seek to be unified in our homes—husbands and wives, parents and children—and unified in our churches. That we will esteem others better than ourselves as we have the mind of Christ. And I pray universally, as believers who may not be in direct contact in the same church but as part of the same body, that we extend grace to one another. And may we esteem others better than ourselves. May we have the mind of Christ. May we stand firm with thanksgiving, praying always. And again, may we stand firm in Jesus Christ.

Questions for Reflection and Discussion

1. Instead of being anxious, what does Paul tell us to do, and what is the result (see 4:6–7)?

2. What did Paul tell us he could do through Christ in His strength (see v. 13)?
   a. Nothing
   b. Some things
   c. All things
   d. None of the above

Notes on Today's Bible Reading

Colossae at the Time of Paul's Imprisonment

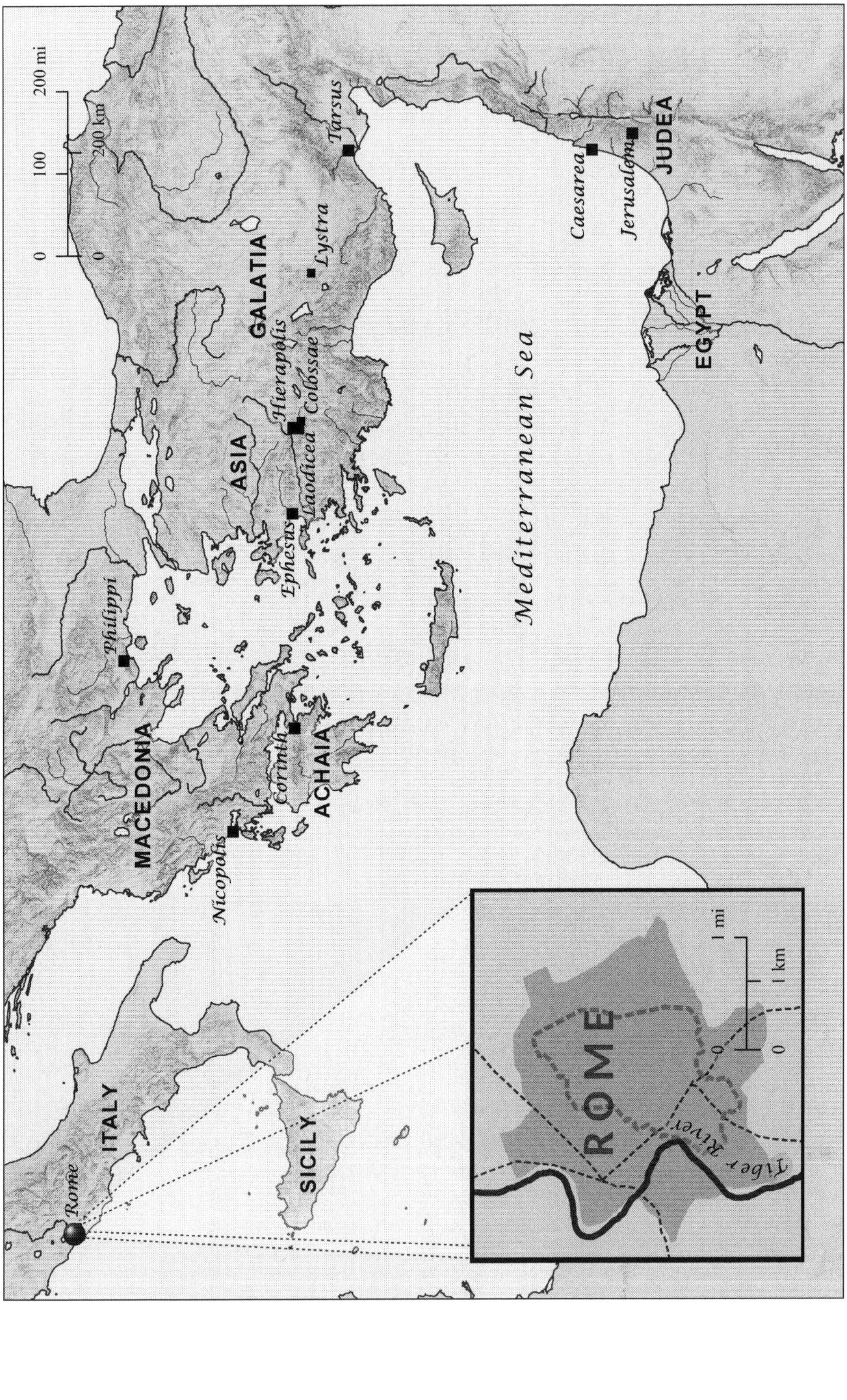

— Day 12 —

Colossians 1–2

Verse of the Day

> Beware lest anyone cheat you through philosophy and empty deceit, according to the tradition of men, according to the basic principles of the world, and not according to Christ.
>
> — *Colossians 2:8*

Please read the entire Scripture selection in your own Bible and highlight or underline verses that stand out to you before you read the observations and engage the questions below.

Today we begin Colossians, the third of the four prison letters in our Bibles that Paul wrote during imprisonment in Rome around AD 61–62. All the prison letters, while sharing some elements in common, have a distinct focus. This letter is filled with one of the foundational truths of the faith, which is the preeminence of Christ. That doctrinal truth sets the stage for addressing the false and deceptive teaching that Christians in Colossae were propagating and following. Before we begin our study of the letter, let us consider the background and an overview of Colossians.

Background

Colossae was an old Phrygian city located in the Lycus Valley in the Roman province of Asia Minor (modern-day Turkey). While it was once a thriving commercial center known for its trade routes and especially its red wool industry, Colossae declined in prominence with the advent of Roman rule. Specifically, when they built the Via Egnatia, the new road bypassed Colossae and diverted trade to Laodicea and Hierapolis. Though it had been overshadowed by those nearby cities, Colossae was ethnically and religiously diverse with Greeks, Jews, and Romans making up the population who needed the gospel.

Overview

Interestingly, Paul wrote to believers in a Colossian church that he didn't start in a city he never visited. Yet in the providence of God, Paul met a man from Colossae named Epaphras and led him to the Lord during his three-year ministry in Ephesus. Then Epaphras took the gospel back to Colossae and helped start a church. Fast forward a few years, and Epaphras came to Rome to visit Paul and reported that the church there was having problems. The cultural melting pot in Colossae apparently led to religious pressures on the church to blend the Christian faith with competing beliefs, practices, and philosophies. Consequently, Paul's letter addressed what appeared to be the first known heresy in the church. A syncretic practice was beginning to emerge combining the teachings of Christ with existing thought systems, such as Greek philosophy, Judaism, and asceticism, which is a form of self-denial. It's not, however, rooted in the truth but rather in self. And then there was an early form of Gnosticism, a heresy that blended Jewish legalism with Greek philosophical concepts, particularly the belief that matter is inherently evil and that salvation comes through special knowledge (*gnosis*) beyond what was given through the Scripture. It follows that Gnostics held a heretical view of Jesus, denying His incarnation in a physical body, thus rejecting the biblical doctrine of His full deity and humanity, which Paul addressed in the first two chapters of Colossians.

Paul's writings in this letter followed the pattern of his other letters, the first half dealing with doctrine and the second half focusing on the practical application of the Christian doctrine. The outline is fairly simple:

- Chapter 1 proclaims the preeminence of Christ over all creation and salvation.
- Chapter 2 declares the preeminence of Christ over all worldly philosophies and systems.
- Chapter 3/part 1 applies the preeminence of Christ to our attitudes and actions as followers of Christ.
- Chapter 3/part 2 and chapter 4 apply the preeminence of Christ to our relationships at home, at work, and in the world.

Commentary

In the first two chapters, Paul urged believers to exalt Christ as preeminent and warned against allowing substitutes to cheat them. Our key verse is Colossians 2:8: "Beware lest anyone cheat you through philosophy and empty deceit, according to the tradition of men, according to the basic principles of the world, and not according to Christ." With that, let's begin in Colossians 1:3: "We give thanks to the God and Father of our Lord Jesus Christ, praying always for you." Paul was quite good about encouraging his people and reminding them of his prayers on their behalf.

Look at Colossians 1:4–6: "since we heard of your faith in Christ Jesus and of your love for all the saints; because of the hope which is laid up for you in heaven, of which you heard before in the word of the truth of the gospel, which has come to you, as it has also in all the world, and is bringing forth fruit, as it is also among you since the day you heard and knew the grace of God in truth." You see, the gospel of Jesus Christ changes lives. It bears fruit. Then in verses 7–8 Paul moved on to the occasion for his writing them: "as you also learned from Epaphras, our dear fellow servant, who is a faithful minister of Christ on your behalf, who also declared to us your love in the Spirit." Epaphras was the messenger who had shared what was happening in Colossae.

As noted earlier, Paul had the habit of affirming his people and letting them know that he thanked God for them. That's encouraging! And Paul also was very good about praying for those to whom he wrote. Again, Paul was a prayer warrior and prayed fervently for these churches. He had the heart of a pastor, and we see this in verses 9–12. He prayed for God to provide for them. Look at Colossians 1:9: "For this reason we also, since the day we heard it, do not cease to pray for you, and to ask that you may be filled with the knowledge of His will in all wisdom and spiritual understanding." That's how we defeat a lie; we pray for a release of the truth. Let's continue in verses 10–12: "That you may walk worthy of the Lord, fully pleasing Him, being fruitful in every good work and increasing in the knowledge of God; strengthened with all might, according to His glorious power, for all patience and longsuffering with joy; giving thanks to the Father who has qualified us to be partakers of the inheritance of the saints in the light."

Paul prayed for them to adhere to essentials of the Christian life, and his words of wisdom apply to us as well. First, walk worthy of the Lord. If you are a follower of Jesus Christ, live like it, which pleases the Lord. Remember what Jesus said in John 14:15: "If you love Me, keep My commandments." James 2:17 says, "Thus also faith by itself, if it does not have works, is dead." Second, be fruitful. Our lives should bear fruit for the kingdom of God. Third, increase in knowledge. We should be growing in our knowledge and understanding of the truth through the Holy Spirit, which means we must be filled with the Spirit, as Paul told the Ephesians. And fourth, give thanks. Here was a guy in prison for serving the Lord, and he reminded them to give thanks to God the Father, who through Jesus Christ delivered them—and us—from the power of darkness. Paul was pointing to the big picture, the eternal picture. Too often we get stuck with a snapshot of today, and we fail to be thankful to God. And when we fail to be thankful, that robs us of our joy and our peace.

Paul introduced the traits that should mark a follower of Christ, and he returned to this again in Colossians 3–4. As he talked about these characteristics, he then turned to the preeminence of Christ. When you grab hold of the truth, other things—the philosophies, the mysticisms, and all the other "isms"—can't get a foothold in you. Paul took on the Gnostics and spoke to the divinity of Christ in His role in creation. Paul presented a profound hymn about Christ's supremacy. Let's look at it in Colossians 1:15–18:

> He is the image of the invisible God, the firstborn over all creation. For by Him all things were created that are in heaven and that are on earth, visible and invisible, whether thrones or dominions or principalities or powers. All things were created through Him and for Him. And He is before all things, and in Him all things consist. And He is the

> head of the body, the church, who is the beginning, the firstborn from the dead, that in all things He may have the preeminence. For it pleased the Father that in Him all the fullness should dwell, and by Him to reconcile all things to Himself, by Him, whether things on earth or things in heaven, having made peace through the blood of His cross.

There are incredible truths in these verses: The exalted Christ uniquely reveals the identity of the invisible God as the firstborn over all creation and the agent and goal of creation. He is the head of the church and the reconciler of all things through His blood shed on the cross.

Note how Paul applied these lofty truths to verses 21–23: "And you, who once were alienated and enemies in your mind by wicked works, yet now He has reconciled in the body of His flesh through death, to present you holy, and blameless, and above reproach in His sight—if indeed you continue in the faith, grounded and steadfast, and are not moved away from the hope of the gospel which you heard, which was preached to every creature under heaven, of which I, Paul, became a minister." Paul reminded the Colossians that they were once alienated from God but were reconciled through Christ's death. They must continue in the faith, firmly grounded in the hope of the gospel.

Next we come to chapter 2, where Paul took on the philosophies of man, making clear that the knowledge of Christ is preeminent above all things. Look at verses 6–8: "As you therefore have received Christ Jesus the Lord, so walk in Him, rooted and built up in Him and established in the faith, as you have been taught, abounding in it with thanksgiving. Beware lest anyone cheat you through philosophy and empty deceit, according to the tradition of men, according to the basic principles of the world, and not according to Christ." The empty-headed philosophies of man are fool's gold. They're counterfeit. Basically, Paul said, "Don't be tricked into an imitation of the truth. Embrace the real thing, Jesus Christ."

Now you might ask, "How are we cheated through these things?" Well, let me give you one example. In our society, biblical truth has been removed or pushed from public spaces. Back in 1962 and 1963, the Bible and prayer were essentially removed from our public schools because we were told those spaces needed to be neutral. Need I ask how that neutrality has worked out? There is no such thing as moral neutrality. Christians were tricked into exchanging the transcendent truth of God for a knockoff of man. And that's left generations empty and without purpose. Look at Colossians 2:9–10: "For in Him dwells all the fullness of the Godhead bodily; and you are complete in Him, who is the head of all principality and power."

In 2:11–23, Paul took on legalism, mysticism, and asceticism. Believers in Christ share in a spiritual circumcision and baptism that is superior to that mandated by the law, which did not have the power to save, only to condemn. Yet Christ took that "handwriting of requirements" and nailed it to His cross (v. 14). Consequently, Paul declared, "So let no one judge you in food or in drink, or regarding a festival or a new moon or sabbaths, which are a shadow of things to come, but the substance is of Christ" (vv. 16–17). In other words, don't let these legalists cheat you out of your freedom in Christ. Then in verses 18–19, Paul warned of going after the mystics who delight in false humility, worship of angels, and speculative philosophy fueled by pride. They are in reality disconnected from Christ, who is sufficient in and of Himself. In verses 20–21, Paul concluded by taking on the ascetics by reminding the Colossian church that if they died with Christ to worldly principles, they should not submit to human regulations that are powerless to restrain sinful desires because they cannot change the heart. Only Christ can transform, and He does so completely when we surrender to Him as Lord.

While it may not be packaged the same way as it was back then, Satan continues to infiltrate the church with false and deceptive teaching, with the goal of robbing the church of its effectiveness and individual believers of the peace and the assurance that comes from trusting in the simple but profound truth of God's Word. It is all laid out for us in God's Word, and it is as simple as it is sublime. As Paul wrote in Romans 10:9–11: "That if you confess with your mouth the Lord Jesus and believe in your heart that God has raised Him from the dead, you will be saved. For with the heart one believes unto righteousness, and with the mouth confession is made unto salvation. For the Scripture says, 'Whoever believes on Him will not be put to shame.'" That's it. Period. Full stop. The gospel is here for us. We don't need to add to it. We're not to take away from it. We're to embrace it. Embrace the truth and don't be cheated with a lie. The exalted Christ is to be preeminent over all these worldly philosophies and systems.

Questions for Reflection and Discussion

1. How is Christ described in Colossians 1:15–19?
   a. Image of the invisible God and Creator of all things
   b. Head of the church
   c. Firstborn from the dead and fullness of God
   d. Reconciler of all things through the cross
   e. All of the above

2. How did Christ cancel the "handwriting of requirements that was against us, which was contrary to us" (see 2:14)?

Notes on Today's Bible Reading

— Day 13 —
Colossians 3–4

Verse of the Day

> Continue earnestly in prayer, being vigilant in it with thanksgiving.
>
> — *Colossians 4:2*

Please read the entire Scripture selection in your own Bible and highlight or underline verses that stand out to you before you read the observations and engage the questions below.

Our key verse today is Colossians 4:2: "Continue earnestly in prayer, being vigilant in it with thanksgiving." So far in our study of the letter the apostle Paul wrote to the Colossians, we've looked at the preeminence of Christ in creation, in the systems of this world, and in our lives in general. Today, we will finish up the letter, and in the last chapter and a half, Paul focused on the preeminence of Christ in our relationships. The key truth that we are going to unpack is this: If we are followers of Jesus Christ, then He will and should be preeminent in our relationships with others. That includes in the home, in the workplace, and in the world. Those relationships should all reflect the fact that He is preeminent in our lives.

Before we get into that topic, let's explore the first part of Colossians 3. This chapter transitions from theological foundations to practical Christian living. First, Paul focused on identity in Christ, urging believers to "seek those things which are above, where Christ is, sitting at the right hand of God" (v. 1b) because "Christ . . . is our life" (v. 4). Then Paul turned our attention to the need to "put to death" the sinful behaviors of the flesh (vv. 5–7) and "put off" the old self with its bad attitudes and speech (vv. 8–9). Next Paul urged believers to "put on" the new self in Christ (vv. 10–17). Note that we are called to "clothe" ourselves with compassion, kindness, humility, gentleness, and patience. Peace and gratitude should rule our hearts, and the Word of Christ should saturate our lives. Forgiveness and love should be the foundation of our relationships.

Speaking of our relationships, now let's focus on the preeminence of Christ in that arena. Paul's discussion began in the wedded home. Look at Colossians 3:18: "Wives, submit to your own husbands, as is fitting in the Lord." Now, this is a controversial statement in the twenty-first century. In fact, a few years ago Southern Baptists put this into their statement of faith, the Baptist Faith and Message. It upset people: "Those Baptists are so backward that they're calling upon their wives to submit to their husbands." It was as if this was some misogynistic, throw-back Neanderthal thought. No, this is the Word of God. Don't worry, it also speaks to the men, but Paul started with the women, the wives. And I can tell you this: If men live according to the Scripture, as Christ has called us to live, women will have no concern submitting to that type of a sacrificially loving husband.

What does it mean to *submit*? Basically, it means to follow the leadership of your husband, providing he is following the Lord. The Lord is not going to call you to do something that is counter to

His Word. He is not going to call you to be in a relationship that is abusive or harmful. Notice the qualification: "as is fitting in the Lord." Ephesians 5:22–24 amplifies this: "Wives, submit to your own husbands, as to the Lord. For the husband is head of the wife, as also Christ is head of the church; and He is the Savior of the body. Therefore, just as the church is subject to Christ, so let the wives be to their own husbands in everything." Wives are to submit to the leadership. Now, whether we like it or not, the men are called to be the leaders of the home. To submit means that wives should respect their husbands. Ephesians 5:33 says, "Nevertheless let each one of you in particular so love his own wife as himself, and let the wife see that she respects her husband." What does it mean to respect? It means to have reverence. In Titus 2:4, Paul wrote, "That they admonish the young women to love their husbands, to love their children." We're to love. And wives are to love their husbands and to be devoted to them.

Paul then turned his attention to the husbands in Colossians 3:19: "Husbands, love your wives and do not be bitter toward them." The word translated "bitter" means to be irritated. Don't be irritated at your wife. Don't let things build up to where you are irritated with your wife. He said instead to love her. Ephesians 5:25 says, "Husbands, love your wives, just as Christ also loved the church and gave Himself for her." He's not talking about the Hollywood type of love that is a feeling that comes and goes. He's talking about the holy matrimony type love. For better or for worse, for sickness and in health. See, the standard is not what Hollywood creates. The standard is what the cross created. And that is, Jesus loved us so much that He died on a cross. A husband who is loving in the nature of Christ will not be seeking to fulfill himself in the marriage relationship, but rather he will be giving to fulfill his wife.

Men, it's time that we grow up and be men, and that we, as the head of the home, are giving to our wives and not taking from our wives. You see, when you love as Christ loved the church, your wife will have no problem submitting to your leadership and respecting you as the head of the home.

If we followed the design of the One who created marriage, maybe we wouldn't have all these problems. So I make no apologies for what the Word of God says. It is relevant to us today. We should continually hold up the standard God has given us. The design of marriage is abundantly clear. It is one man and one woman in a relationship for life, and that is what we should aspire to do. And note that God's design for the family begins with marriage. Cohabitation is not God's design for the home. God's Word is proven day in and day out in the society around us as believers. And again, Paul was writing to believers. I know what the culture is saying, and I know what Hollywood is portraying. But, folks, if we want to live a life of spiritual significance for the kingdom of God, we need to do it according to the Word of God.

Next, Paul addressed children. Look at Colossians 3:20: "Children, obey your parents in all things, for this is well pleasing to the Lord." This is basic. Children in the home are to obey their parents. Obviously, this does not speak to middle-aged, adult children still tied on the apron strings of Mom and living on Dad's dime. At some point everyone needs to grow up and get out on their own. However, if children are to obey their parents when they are young, they are to honor their parents when they're grown. Look what it says in Exodus 20:12: "Honor your father and your mother, that your days may be long upon the land which the LORD your God is giving you." If you obey your parents then you honor your parents, you will enjoy the blessing of a long life. You know, part of that just plays its way out. If you disobey your parents and you reject their counsel, you're going to end up in trouble and life will not only be miserable; in many cases it will be short. Finally, adult children should care for their parents when they get old. Jesus called out the Pharisees for trying to skirt this responsibility under the guise of religious devotion, but it was a sham (Matt. 15:3–9). Our responsibility to our parents only ends with their deaths.

Before he left the subject of the wedded home, Paul wrote specifically to fathers. Notice He didn't talk to mothers; they usually get it right instinctively. He addressed fathers. Colossians 3:21 says, "Fathers, do not provoke your children, lest they become discouraged." Notice he transitioned from the positive to the negative. He told the parent, the fathers in particular, not to do something. That usually indicates that fathers are prone to do something. And he said, "Don't do it." Don't perpetually find fault in your children. And I know as a father of five wonderful children whom I'm blessed to have, I've been down that road. All of us fathers have. How many of you have been down that road and know the pitfalls and the consequences? You and I want the best for our children, and I think sometimes we are overly critical. I know I have been wanting them to make the right decisions and the right choices and not to do certain things. Basically, Paul said, "Don't provoke them to wrath. Don't always find fault. Encourage them. Don't discourage your children."

Also, we're not to discourage them in their walk with the Lord. I think fathers have discouraged their children's faith walk because they lack integrity. Our walk has to match our talk. Fathers, if you are putting on a spiritual front, let me tell you that your children will see through it. They will see that you lack integrity, and their interpretation of Christianity will be that it is a fraud. It's a fake.

You and I should live authentically. That doesn't mean perfect. I said authentically, which means when we make mistakes, we admit it. I've had to go to my children to apologize for not doing something the right way as a father. And you know what, dads? That's OK. It's OK to admit that we're human and that we make mistakes. Don't discourage your children from their walk with the Lord by lacking integrity.

We should not discourage them but, rather, encourage them to be who God has created them to be. Too many fathers want to live their lives out through their children. God hasn't given you children to be like you. God has given you children for you to train up. They're His. And we have the great privilege of, for a short period of time, being their shepherd and being their coach and their tutor and training them and equipping them. But God has uniquely called each and every one of them to do something for Him. What a father should be doing is looking and praying over their kids. I say, "Lord, what is it that you would have for them to do? Show me so that I can help them in that area." So, as fathers, we need to be looking at how we can help our children be all that God has created them to be.

Then we turn from the home to the workplace. The Word of God speaks to how we should conduct ourselves at work. Colossians 3:22–24 says, "Bondservants, obey in all things your master's according to the flesh, not with eyeservice, as men-pleasers, but in sincerity of heart, fearing God. And whatever you do, do it heartily, as to the Lord and not to men, knowing that from the Lord you will receive the reward of the inheritance; for you serve the Lord Christ."

First, Paul spoke to employees. He said, obey the boss. Some might object: "You don't know my boss. He's a tyrant!" I've had a few of those. And I've learned the most and developed some great skills from some of the most difficult bosses I've had. Part of it, however, is I've learned there's something in me that bristles up, and the Lord had to deal with that. So when we are in those difficult situations, working for difficult people, ask, "Lord, what do you want to show me?" On top of this, the quicker we learn, the quicker we can get out of there.

Look what Peter said over in 1 Peter 2: "Servants, be submissive to your masters with all fear, not only to the good and gentle, but also to the harsh. For this is commendable, if because of conscience toward God one endures grief, suffering wrongfully" (vv. 18–19). We must be willing to not just honor and obey the kind, compassionate, and the good people we work for. We have to obey the difficult and the harsh ones too because it is honoring to the Lord.

Paul said not only are we to obey our earthly boss, but we're to fear God. Don't give eyeservice. In other words, don't just work hard when your boss is watching. Know that the Lord is watching. Get your eyes off the clock and put them on Christ. Don't just do what you have to in order to get by. Do your very best. That's what Christians should be doing as employees: working for the Lord and doing their very best for the Lord. I want you to think about this for a moment. If you had a choice, would you rather work for the XYZ company or for the Lord of the universe? Who would you work for? I can tell you, the retirement plan of the Lord of the universe is much better. I mean, who do you think will treat you more fairly and ensure you are rewarded for faithful service?

I discovered a number of years ago that I didn't have to work for a difficult boss. I didn't have to work for a challenging company. I could work for the Lord. Now, it just so happened that He assigned me temporarily at a difficult company with a challenging boss, but

He had a great transfer policy. He moved me to a different location to give me a greater opportunity and more responsibility. And guess what? Even sometimes an increase in my salary because I was working for Him. I wasn't working for a small Fortune 500 company. I was working for the Creator of the universe. Let me tell you how freeing that is. I work at a company with the best benefits. I work at a company that provides the greatest opportunities because I am no longer limited to the bank account of a company. God sent resources in a hundred different ways when I decided to work for the Lord and not simply for an employer. And I do my work as unto the Lord, meaning I'm not waiting for that supervisor to look over my shoulder or that quality control guy to see if I did my job. I'm doing it because I know God in heaven is looking down, and He is a rewarder of those who do well.

Colossians 3:25 says, "But he who does wrong will be repaid for what he has done, and there is no partiality." This means God doesn't see the difference between an employer and an employee. We all work for Him.

In fact, Paul begins to pivot here from employees to addressing the employers in chapter 4. There is no break in the original manuscript between the chapters, but Colossians 4:1 goes on to say, "Masters, give your bondservants what is just and fair, knowing that you also have a Master in heaven." Employers should treat their people with justice and fairness. James 5:4 says, "Indeed the wages of the laborers who mowed your fields, which you kept back by fraud, cry out; and the cries of the reapers have reached the ears of the Lord of Sabaoth." The Lord of hosts—the sovereign One who leads the host of heaven, the armies of heaven—He hears those who have been defrauded by their employers and He says, "Don't do it." Treat them with justice and fairness. I'll tell you this: If more employers conducted business according to biblical principles, we could eliminate most government regulations and agencies. We wouldn't need them. Furthermore, as religious freedom is being pushed from the marketplace, meaning Christians are not allowed to do all for the glory of God, look only for the situation to get worse as the size and demands and cost of government increases. Life would be so much less complicated if we would simply live according to the Word of God.

Back to Colossians 4:1, which says that employers are to operate under authority. That means we operate with humility, knowing we will give an account to God for everything that we do. And when we operate under God, we recognize that we are accountable to God. In fact, this is what was meant in 1956 when we changed the pledge of our nation to add "Under God." It was acknowledging that our leaders, our government, does not operate as it wants, but rather as it ought under the authority of God. You see, when a nation rejects the authority of God, as our nation has increasingly, they end up with despots like Russia's Putin, China's Xi, or North Korea's Rocket Man. The authority of God is over all of us, each and every one.

Paul then pivots from the workplace to the world. Christ should be preeminent in our relationships outside the church. Let's continue in Colossians 4:5–6: "Walk in wisdom toward those who are outside, redeeming the time. Let your speech always be with grace, seasoned with salt, that you may know how you ought to answer each one." We are to live with integrity, meaning that as Christians the world should see us as what we say we are, followers of Jesus.

I know many are hesitant to even attempt to live out biblical truth because they're afraid others will say, "You didn't live up to your commitment." True, we all have feet of clay. We are all sinners.

We live in a fallen world. Nobody is perfect, not even Christians. Only Jesus is perfect. Yet when we realize we have a world that is watching, this vast cloud of witnesses, it should not drive us away from the truth. Rather, it should drive us to our knees that we might live according to the truth. We're to walk with integrity. We should not give the world anymore of a reason to be dismissive of the message of salvation that comes from Jesus Christ. The world has always been skeptical, and the world has always been filled with those who are indifferent and intolerant—even some are filled with outright hate toward Christ and the gospel message. We are not to give them anymore of a reason by lacking integrity in our Christian walk.

Note that Paul said that we are to look for opportunities, "redeeming the time." In other words, we should be praying for those opportunities to share the message of the gospel and looking for opportunities to minister to those who are hurting. When we live with integrity, although imperfect, those with whom we work are going to see it. And when they are in trouble, they will turn to us. I can guarantee it. I've seen it a thousand times. And we should be prepared for those opportunities.

Let's go back and consider verses 2–4. Here Paul asked for people to pray for him so that he would speak as he ought. And so I have no hesitation asking for people to help me do the same. And then he said we're to speak the truth with love. Even when the truth is difficult, when someone asks us for advice and we know what the Word of God says, we need to speak with clarity and with love. Still, remember: We cannot hedge on the Word of God. We need to be prepared.

Consider what 1 Peter 3:15a says, "But sanctify the Lord God in your hearts." How do you do that? You spend time with Him.

You spend time in prayer. You spend time in His Word. And Peter went on to say, "and always be ready to give a defense to everyone who asks you a reason for the hope that is in you." When a coworker comes to you and says, "How is it that you kind of get the short straw all the time, but you're still smiling about it? Are you sick? What's wrong with you? Are you a glutton for punishment?" Just say, "No, I work for the greatest Employer in all creation. I work for Jesus. And let me tell you about Him." We need to be prepared to speak about the hope that is within us.

Now that we have looked at how these relationships should work in the wedded home, in the workplace, and in the world around us, let us consider the way these often difficult relationships can be brought under the preeminence of Christ. How do we do this? Colossians 4:2 says, "Continue earnestly in prayer, being vigilant in it with thanksgiving." We need to be persevering in prayer, mindful of the preeminence of Christ. I cannot stress this enough: Set aside a time every day to spend alone in prayer, and that's literally what Paul talked about. Make sure you have a dedicated time alone with God. Get away from social media and talk radio, away from the disruptions and cares of the world, so that you can persevere in prayer and be reminded of the preeminence of Christ. When all of the things in this world are going on, we need to be reminded that Christ is over all, including in our own lives. James 5:16 says, "Confess your trespasses to one another, and pray for one another, that you may be healed. The effective, fervent prayer of a righteous man avails much." You see, prayer keeps us dependent upon God.

I remember a number of years ago a girl, who was five or six years old, was acting up in church, and I think it was her mom who picked her up and took her out back to the church foyer. (When I started going to church at about six years old, I thought the foyer was a place used only for parents to spank their kids.) So the mother was carrying this little girl who had been misbehaving toward the back door. And just as she was about to open the door, at the top of her lungs, she screamed out, "People, pray for me!" Prayer is not just for those moments of desperation. We are to be persevering in prayer. And then Paul said to be watchful in prayer, meaning watching as if on guard duty. Like Nehemiah when he heard of the enemy's plots and schemes. Remember how Nehemiah prayed and set a watch? That is what Paul was saying here. We are to watch against the enemy getting a foothold, the old nature creeping in and taking over. We need to pray that God will change us, but then we must take responsibility to watch and pray.

Let me ask you, does your marriage honor God? It should. Pray and ask God what needs to change in you and then set out to change it. Get counseling if you need it, but just warn your spouse beforehand. Does your relationship with your children honor God? Pray and ask God if something needs to change and then do it. Does your reputation at work honor God? If not, pray and ask God how you can change it and then do it. Do you have integrity before a watching world? If not, confess and pray and ask God to use the Holy Spirit in your life to change what needs to be changed and then do it.

Then finally Paul said this, basically: "Be grateful in prayer. Be grateful to God, our provider." I want to remind you again, Paul wrote this from prison, yet he's telling the Colossians to be grateful in all things. In 1 Thessalonians 5:18 he said, "in everything give thanks; for this is the will of God in Christ Jesus for you." One of the ways that we are reminded of the preeminence of Christ in our relationships is by giving thanks, even in difficult situations and difficult relationships. You see, when we give thanks, what we are actually doing is agreeing with God's plan over the current realities. I'm not saying we are to ignore realities. I'm saying that we are to say in faith, "God, thank You for this relationship that is going to be changed and aligned with Your Word. Thank You for the work that You're doing in me. Thank You for this relationship. Thank You for that relationship. I know it's challenging right now, but Lord, I thank You that all things are under the preeminence and the authority of Jesus Christ."

How important are our relationships? Relationships are everything, starting with our relationship with Jesus Christ. From there, as we allow Him to have preeminence in our lives, we can enrich the lives of others, our own lives will have significance, and most importantly, they will bring glory to God. But our relationships with others will never, ever be what God intended them to be until we first begin a relationship with Jesus Christ. He must be preeminent.

Questions for Reflection and Discussion

1. What does Paul say about our work life (see 3:23–24)?
   a. If we have a terrible boss, do the minimum.
   b. If we have a low-paying job, cut corners.
   c. If customers are ungrateful, slack on the job.
   d. None of the above.

2. What did Paul encourage about our speech (see 4:6)?

Notes on Today's Bible Reading

— Day 14 —
Philemon

Verse of the Day

> So if you consider me your partner, receive him as you would receive me.
>
> — *Philemon 1:17*

Please read the entire Scripture selection in your own Bible and highlight or underline verses that stand out to you before you read the observations and engage the questions below.

Today we will look at the brief letter of Philemon. Our key verse is Philemon 1:17: "If then you count me as a partner, receive him as you would me." This is the last of the four epistles, or letters, Paul wrote when he was in prison in Rome the first time. These were written between AD 61 and 62.

Background and Overview

The letter to Philemon is different than the other letters in several ways. First, it's a personal letter. Philemon was a leader in the church in Colossae. In fact, it is believed that a church met in his home. There were no church buildings at this time. In fact, it was the early third century before there were actual church buildings, so people met in homes. Another different aspect of this letter is that it did not address doctrine, as Paul did in his other letters. There are certainly principles here, but there are no doctrinal statements. I wonder whether Paul would be amazed that millions of people have read this personal letter that he wrote to Philemon about his slave Onesimus, who had run away. Yet in the providence of God, Onesimus encountered Paul in Rome, was converted to Christ by Paul's teaching of the gospel, and now was preparing to return to his master, Philemon. We don't know all the details of the backstory. What we do know is that this letter shows us the character of Paul, which reflects the humility and the compassion of Christ and presents us with a model worthy of imitation.

Commentary

Let's begin in Philemon 1:1–2: "Paul, a prisoner of Christ Jesus, and Timothy our brother, to Philemon our beloved friend and fellow laborer, to the beloved Apphia, Archippus our fellow soldier, and to the church in your house." Apphia is believed to be Philemon's wife. Archippus is thought to be his son. Note that Paul rightfully recognized Apphia as the one hosting the church in her home because I'm sure she was the one who did most of the work. You know, many husbands commit to things, but it is the wives who must carry them out. At least that's been my experience. Also note Paul's political incorrectness here. He referred to Archippus as a fellow soldier. Recognize it or not, like it or not, we're in a spiritual war. And if we are truly following Jesus Christ, we're spiritual warriors for the kingdom of God. That means there will be conflict, and we must be as soldiers. As Paul wrote about in Ephesians, we've got to have on the armor.

Now let's read Philemon 1:3–4, "Grace to you and peace from God our Father and the Lord Jesus Christ. I thank my God, making mention of you always in my prayers." We see this repeatedly in Paul's letters, and I do not believe it was an empty greeting or a throwaway line. He said, "I'm praying for you." Unfortunately, I think that may be used by some today when we encounter someone who's struggling or having challenges. We say, "I'll be praying for you." That's great if we follow through, but I'm afraid far too often it's not the case. It is something we should strive for. We need to be intentional, focused, and effective in our prayer lives. James wrote that the effective, fervent prayer of a righteous man avails much, and we need to be praying for one another.

Continuing in verses 5–7: "hearing of your love and faith which you have toward the Lord Jesus and toward all the saints, that the sharing of your faith may become effective by the acknowledgment of every good thing which is in you in Christ Jesus. For we have great joy and consolation in your love, because the hearts of the saints have been refreshed by you, brother." Paul's purpose in this letter, as we will see, was to appeal to Philemon for grace and forgiveness for Onesimus, Philemon's runaway slave. Apparently, Onesimus took something that didn't belong to him (see v. 18) and went to Rome but then encountered Paul. Some basic human relationship skills were being employed here by Paul in how he approached Philemon. Notice how Paul built on his relationship with and was concerned for Philemon before he moved into the heart of the matter. So part of that was letting Philemon know that he cared about him. He had his best interests at heart.

Now notice verses 8–9: "Therefore, though I might be very bold in Christ to command you what is fitting, yet for love's sake I rather appeal to you—being such a one as Paul, the aged, and now also a prisoner of Jesus Christ." Paul had matured in the faith in his leadership, and he was not demanding or forcing, but he was leading. Look at verse 10: "I appeal to you for my son Onesimus, whom I have begotten while in my chains." What this means is that Paul led Onesimus to the Lord. And by the way, as the name Onesimus means "profitable" or "useful," there's a play on words: "who once was unprofitable to you, but now is profitable to you and to me. I am sending him back. You therefore receive him, that is, my own heart, whom I wished to keep with me, that on your behalf he might minister to me in my chains for the gospel" (vv. 11–13). So basically, Paul said, "He's profitable to both you and me. He's profitable to you because he's profitable to me."

Next consider Philemon 1:14–16: "But without your consent I wanted to do nothing, that your good deed might not be by compulsion, as it were, but voluntary. For perhaps he departed for a while for this purpose, that you might receive him forever, no longer as a slave but more than a slave—a beloved brother, especially to me but how much more to you, both in the flesh and in the Lord." Notice what Paul said here is the same message as Romans 8:28: "And we know that all things work together for good to those who love God, to those who are the called according to His purpose." Admittedly, this whole set of circumstances did not start well, and the intentions were not good. But despite his rebellious actions, Onesimus had repented and come to know the Lord, and Paul was telling Philemon, "Now he's going to be with you forever, in eternity as a brother. So, he departed. When he ran away from you, he was not a brother. He came to me, and he came to know the Lord. Now he's coming back to you as a brother in the Lord, and you're going to be with him forever." So God had transformed this man, and now he was living up to his name—he was profitable, beneficial.

Let's continue in Philemon 1:17–18: "If then you count me as a partner, receive him as you would me. But if he has wronged you or owes anything, put that on my account." Here Paul, a prisoner whom I doubt had much to his name, told a very wealthy man, Philemon, "If Onesimus owes you anything, put it on my tab. I'll take care of it." In a way, when we look closely at this, Paul was a picture of Jesus Christ. Like Onesimus, we are slaves to sin and we're on the run. The penalty for a slave who ran away was death. And Paul, like Jesus did for us, became an advocate for Onesimus and said, "Put whatever he owes on my account." That's exactly what Jesus did for us.

In verse 19, Paul began to wrap up his letter: "I, Paul, am writing with my own hand. I will repay—not to mention to you that you owe me even your own self besides." It was through the teaching of Paul, in either Ephesus or Colossae, that Philemon heard the gospel and became a believer. Then read verses 20–22: "Yes, brother, let me have joy from you in the Lord; refresh my heart in the Lord. Having confidence in your obedience, I write to you, knowing that you will do even more than I say. But, meanwhile, also prepare a guest room for me, for I trust that through your prayers I shall be granted to you." Paul was, basically, "Look, I know you're praying for me. All the saints are praying for me, and I have faith that I'm going to be coming to see you. So make that room ready."

Unfortunately, we don't have the outcome of this letter recorded in Scripture. We don't know what happened with Philemon and Onesimus. There is, however, speculation that Ignatius, a bishop of Antioch, wrote about Onesimus in the early second century.

Ignatius referred to an Onesimus, the bishop at the church of Ephesus.[6] Consequently, some believe this is the same Onesimus Philemon released, who then went to aid Paul, was trained up like Timothy as a church leader, and ultimately became the bishop at Ephesus. True or not, this is the way God works, and that is the power of the gospel.

Today we conclude our study of the prison letters of Paul. In Ephesians, he urged us to stand firm in the Lord and keep on standing. In Philippians, he encouraged us to rejoice in the Lord always regardless of our circumstances. In Colossians, he called on us to exalt Christ to the place of preeminence in every area of life. And in Philemon, Paul pleaded with us to model Jesus in forgiving and setting others free so that we too might experience freedom. I pray that the Lord motivates you by these ancient words of Paul written from prison, and that the same Holy Spirit who inspired him fills and empowers you to take these words and live by them, for the glory of God.

Questions for Reflection and Discussion

1. What did Onesimus do that offended Philemon?
   a. Called him names
   b. Questioned his authority
   c. Ran away
   d. None of the above

2. What did Paul request of Philemon regarding Onesimus?

Notes on Today's Bible Reading

Appendix 1:
Stand on the Word Bible Reading Plan

Visit frc.org/Bible for our chronological journey through the Bible that we call "Stand on the Word." We encourage you to spend time reading and studying the Bible because it is literally "God-breathed" (2 Tim. 3:16 NIV); it is God's very words to us. The Bible answers the big questions, such as, Why am I here? Where did I come from? Where am I going (life after death)? If God is good, why does evil and suffering exist? The Bible not only answers these big questions; it offers practical advice in areas such as, How can I deal with feelings of fear or anger or guilt? How can I forgive when I cannot forget? What should I look for in a spouse? How can I have a successful marriage? How can I be a good parent? What is my spiritual gift and place in the church? What is my stewardship responsibility as a citizen? We learned the verse in Bible school, "Your word is a lamp to my feet and a light to my path" (Ps. 119:105). God's Word shows us the way forward in any area of life and on every question we face.

The Stand on the Word Bible Reading Plan takes us through the Bible chronologically. In other words, each reading takes us through the Bible as events occurred in history as far as it is possible. Here is how it works for our family. At the same time each morning, whether I am at home, in Washington, or some foreign country, I send my wife and children a morning greeting along with a reminder of the passage for the day. The text includes two questions related to the reading. The questions are designed to help in content retention, serve as an accountability tool, and provide for discussion.

The two-year plan does not have a Sunday passage. Instead, it provides an outline for a family discussion that can be done on Sunday afternoon or evening. Our family has incorporated the discussion into our Sunday lunch, which follows a biblical model of life enriching conversations over a meal. The weekly discussion time begins with a spiritual leader asking each person individually for one or two insights or truths they gained from their reading during the week and how those truths apply to our lives. After everyone else shares, the father or group leader can lead a short discussion of one of the passages that was read during the week and how it applies to our lives here and now. It is also a time for them to ask questions.

By the way, you don't have to have all the answers. If you don't know, tell them so, then talk to your pastor or other trusted person with Bible knowledge. If your children start asking questions, that suggests they are thinking about what they are reading.

Reading God's Word will help you establish a fruitful walk with the God who made you and loves you. Whether you are single or married, this plan will enable you to lead your friends and family in daily reading God's Word. The added benefit is that you will all be reading the same text together. It will amaze you to see how God speaks sometimes in the same ways and at other times in different ways to each of you. Being on this journey together will build a spiritual synergy, a deep bond, and sense of unity and purpose like nothing else! Use it to impart the Word of life. Visit frc.org/Bible to sign up or simply download the Stand Firm App.

Appendix 2:
Prayer: Talking with God

Most Americans say they pray, but not as many pray the way Jesus did and taught His disciples to pray. Fewer, still, really know the power in prayer that God gave us to impact our families, communities, nation, and world. But prayer is our lifeline to God, our means of communicating with our heavenly Father. It develops our relationship—our friendship, fellowship, and intimacy—with Him. In prayer we experience God and are "filled with the Spirit" (Eph. 5:18–21). God uses the prayers of faithful men, women, boys, and girls to heal broken lives and strengthen families, churches, communities, and even nations. He uses our prayers to advance His kingdom on earth (Daniel 9; Acts 4:36)! He wants to so use all believers!

The Essence of Prayer

Prayer is simply talking with God—about anything and everything. He is our Maker, Father, Savior, Provider, and Counselor, our Master, Healer, Guide, and Friend. Christ died for our sins and rose from the dead to sit at the right hand of God the Father, where He is praying for us right now (Heb. 10:12). His Spirit now lives within us and helps us to pray (1 John 4:16).

The Priority of Prayer

Jesus spent time alone with God regularly drawing strength from the Father and seeking His will for every decision (Luke 6:12–13; 22:39–44). His disciples asked Jesus to teach them how to pray (Luke 11:1–13). The apostles knew that prayer and obedience were the keys to Christ's life and ministry and were determined to follow His example: "[W]e will devote ourselves to prayer and to the ministry of the word" (Acts 6:4 ESV). Too few American men pray today, even pastors and leaders! Yet strong praying men are the norm in Scripture. Our families, churches, and nation need men who will make prayer a priority today! (1 Tim. 2:8)

The Practice of Prayer

Scripture teaches, "Pray continually!" (1 Thess. 5:17 NIV); "Praying always" (Eph. 6:18); "Always pray and not give up" (Luke 18:1 NIV). Below are some helps to get you started. No one can beat the Lord's Prayer. It is an outline of key themes to guide our prayer lives:

> "Our Father in heaven,
> hallowed be your name.
> Your kingdom come,
> your will be done,
> on earth as it is in heaven.
> Give us this day our daily bread,
> and forgive us our debts,
> as we also have forgiven our debtors.
> And lead us not into temptation,
> but deliver us from evil." (Matt. 6:9–13 ESV)

In the book of Psalms and throughout Scripture, God has sprinkled prayers: patterns for us to learn from. Here is a simple, popular acronym to help jog our memories:

P-R-A-Y:

- *Praise:* Our Father in heaven, hallowed be your name.
- *Repent:* And forgive us our debts, as we also have forgiven our debtors.
- *Ask:* Give us this day our daily bread, and forgive us our debts, as we also have forgiven our debtors. And lead us not into temptation, but deliver us from evil.
- *Yield:* Your kingdom come, your will be done, on earth as it is in heaven.

Praying Through Scripture

God also talks to us. The Bible is His Word (2 Tim. 2:15; 3:16). Bible in hand, we should pray God's promises back to Him, and claim them for our families, our work, our finances, and our nation (1 Tim. 2:1–8; 1 John 5:14–15).

Scriptures to Pray as a Man: Joshua 1:8; 1 Timothy 3:1–15; 1 Chronicles 12:32; 1 Timothy 6:1–12; 1 Corinthians 16:13; Romans 12:1–21; Micah 6:8; John 4:24; Acts 2:38; 1 Kings 2:2; Husbands: Ephesians 5:25–28; Genesis 2:24; 1 Peter 3:7; Ephesians 4:26–27; Matthew 5:32; Proverbs 5:19; 1 Corinthians 6:18; Fathers: Deuteronomy 4:8–10; 11:18–21; Exodus 34:5–8; Psalm 127:3–5; Matthew 7:11; Ephesians 6:4; Proverbs 22:6; Luke 11:11–12; Hebrews 12:5–7

Scriptures to Pray as a Woman: Matthew 22:36–40; Proverbs 31:30; 1 Peter 3:1–3; Ephesians 5:26; Ephesians 4:15, 29; 1 Timothy 3:11; Ephesians 5:22, 24; 1 Peter 3:1–2; Philippians 4:10– 13;

Philippians 2:3–4; Proverbs 31:12; 1 Corinthians 7:34; Titus 2:3–4; Titus 2:4–5; James 1:19; Ephesians 4:32; 1 Corinthians 7:1–5; Luke 2:37; Colossians 4:2; Proverbs 31:27; 1 Timothy 5:14

Scriptures to Pray for Your Children: Matthew 22:36–40; 2 Timothy 3:15; Psalm 97:10, 38:18; Proverbs 8:13; John 17:15, 10:10; Romans 12:9; Psalm 119:71; Hebrews 12:5–6; Daniel 1:17, 20; Proverbs 1:4; James 1:5; Romans 13:1; Ephesians 6:1–3; Hebrews 13:17; Proverbs 1:10–16, 13:20; 2 Corinthians 6:14–17; Deuteronomy 6; 1 Corinthians 6:18–20; Acts 24:16; 1 Timothy 1:19, 4:1–2; Titus 1:15–16; Psalm 23:4; Deuteronomy 10:12; Matthew 28:18–20; Ephesians 1:3, 4:29; Ephesians 1:16–19; Philippians 1:11; Colossians 1:9; Philippians 1:9–10

Developing Personal Prayer Habits

Rise early each day to pray with opened Bible. Daniel prayed three times daily. Pray whenever you can: as you drive, with your wife, with your children at dinner and before bedtime. You cannot pray too much!

Praying Together with Others

Pray with your spouse regularly. Make time for family prayer. Be part of your church prayer meeting or group. Christ said, "My house shall be called a house of prayer." The apostle Paul instructed Pastor Timothy (1 Tim. 2:1–8) to make prayer the first order of the church, saying prayer is key to peace in the nation. There is nothing like a Spirit-led prayer meeting with people who love the Lord! Praying women have been standing in the prayer gap for decades. Every man must set his heart to become a praying man, lead his family in prayer, and be a strong contributor to the corporate prayer life of his church. We must be leaders in praying for our morally and spiritually troubled, divided nation—and for our national leaders. American Christians simply must respond to God's promise: "If My people who are called by My name will humble themselves, and pray and seek My face, and turn from their wicked ways, then I will hear from heaven, and will forgive their sin and heal their land" (2 Chron. 7:14).

Prayer As Warfare

Jesus described the enemy, the devil, as a thief whose mission is "to steal, and to kill, and to destroy" (John 10:10). Demonic forces are at war against everything good in you, your family, your church, your community, America, and every nation (Eph. 6:10–20).

The devil and his minions are out to thwart the kingdom of God and eliminate righteousness wherever he can. He hates God, hates people, and will use spiritually ignorant and deceived men, women, boys, and girls to do his bidding. Men of God today, like the sons of Issachar in ancient Israel, need to understand the times and know what the church and our nation must do (1 Chron. 12:32). We must pull down Satan's strongholds, wrestle for our families, and use Spirit-led prayer and wisdom to help guide our churches and communities to prevail against the evil onslaught against us (2 Cor. 10:3–5). This is the war of the ages and it is real.

Finally, Determine to Become a Person of Prayer

No matter how long you have been a Christian and may have neglected prayer up until now, you can become a person of prayer starting today. If you have missed the mark, it is not too late. Call upon the Lord, ask His help, and proceed with His guidance. *O Lord, make me a praying person; make me a prayer warrior! In Jesus's name, amen!*

Appendix 3:
How to Share Your Faith

Recent polling from Lifeway Research shows that "only 3 in 10 unchurched Americans (29%) say a Christian has ever shared with them one-on-one how a person becomes a Christian."[7]

Even less are successful in helping someone make a decision to follow Christ. Maybe that is why this whole notion of sharing your faith is so intimidating for many. However, it does not have to be. The best place to start is with your story. Some call it a testimony. In a courtroom, testimony is relied on as part of the evidence in a case. As you are telling your story, you are presenting evidence for how Christ has changed your life for the better. If you are speaking with another man about your faith, think in terms of telling your story in three parts:

1. Your life before you became a follower of Christ.
2. Your encounter with Christ and your decision to follow him as your Savior and Lord.
3. Your life since becoming as a follower of Christ.

The great apostle Paul told his faith story numerous times—several of them are recorded in the Bible. You'll notice these same three parts in Acts 22.

1. Life Before Christ

First of all, notice what Paul said about his life before Christ:

> "I am a Jew, born in Tarsus in Cilicia, but brought up in this city, educated at the feet of Gamaliel according to the strict manner of the law of our fathers, being zealous for God as all of you are this day. I persecuted this Way to the death, binding and delivering to prison both men and women, as the high priest and the whole council of elders can bear me witness. From them I received letters to the brothers, and I journeyed toward Damascus to take those also who were there and bring them in bonds to Jerusalem to be punished." (Acts 22:3–5 ESV)

If there was ever a Jew who was steeped in religion, that Jew was Paul. His religious trophy case was filled to overflowing (v. 3). Over in Philippians 3, he pulled out and dusted off several of them. Then he described his radical commitment to his religion to the point of persecuting followers of Christ (vv. 4–5). Take time to write out what you remember about your life before your life-changing encounter with Christ. Be brief and to the point:

____

____

____

____

____

____

____

____

____

____

2. Encounter with Christ

Paul not only told about his life before Christ, but then he shared his life-changing encounter with Christ:

> "As I was on my way and drew near to Damascus, about noon a great light from heaven suddenly shone around me. And I fell to the ground and heard a voice saying to me, 'Saul, Saul, why are you persecuting me?' And I answered, 'Who are you, Lord?' And he said to me, 'I am Jesus of Nazareth, whom you are persecuting.' Now those who were with me saw the light but did not understand the voice of the one who was speaking to me." (Acts 22:6–9 ESV)

Notice Paul said in verse 9: "Who are you, Lord?" He was told by a heavenly voice: "I am Jesus of Nazareth, whom you are persecuting." What an amazing encounter! Obviously, most people don't get blinded by a light or hear voices from heaven. However, your story of your encounter with Christ is unique, and no doubt it was (and hopefully still is) a powerful experience for you. Take time to write out your encounter with Christ and how you came to make the decision to follow him as Savior and Lord, but don't rush it. Tell what happened in detail:

3. Life-Change After Christ

Paul then began to tell about the changes in his life after his encounter with Christ:

> "And I said, 'What shall I do, Lord?' And the Lord said to me, 'Rise, and go into Damascus, and there you will be told all that is appointed for you to do.' And since I could not see because of the brightness of that light, I was led by the hand by those who were with me, and came into Damascus.
>
> "And one Ananias, a devout man according to the law, well spoken of by all the Jews who lived there, came to me,

> and standing by me said to me, 'Brother Saul, receive your sight.' And at that very hour I received my sight and saw him. And he said, 'The God of our fathers appointed you to know his will, to see the Righteous One and to hear a voice from his mouth; for you will be a witness for him to everyone of what you have seen and heard. And now why do you wait? Rise and be baptized and wash away your sins, calling on his name.'" (Acts 22:10–16 ESV)

In verse 10, Paul asked, basically, "Lord, what next?" and the risen Christ told him, "You will be told all that is appointed for you to do." And then Ananias, another disciple of Jesus, communicated Paul's assignment in verses 13–16, which was basically to give his testimony and tell his story "to all people." Obviously, Paul accepted his assignment and went on to become one of the greatest leaders in the history of the Christian faith, going on missionary journeys, leading multitudes to faith in Jesus, planting churches, ordaining leaders, even giving his testimony to officials in Rome, which was the capital of the ancient world. He also experienced persecution, imprisonment, and finally death for his faith. Again, Paul's story can be intimidating, but it doesn't need to be. Just think about how your life has changed since you began following Christ. Write down some of your thoughts. Remember, you are trying to offer compelling evidence.

Having read how Paul told his faith story, use the outline above and write out yours. Once you have written it, read through it and prayerfully edit it. After you feel good about it, practice sharing it with another trusted and seasoned believer, preferably someone who has successfully helped lead someone else to faith in Christ. Then you may want to go back and edit it again as you may have thought about a better way to communicate it. Finally, pray for God to open a door of opportunity to share your faith story with someone. Pray that the Holy Spirit will prepare the way for you and do only what He can do. At the end of our best efforts to share Christ, it is still up to God and the individual.

Appendix 4:
The Solution to Our Greatest Challenge

What is the greatest challenge facing families and the church today? It is a lack of a biblical worldview. A worldview is the lens through which we view life and the world around us. Having a biblical worldview means the Bible is our lens. Everything in life is filtered through and viewed from a biblical perspective. The problem is that very few can truthfully claim that the Bible is their authoritative point of reference for what they value and how they behave. In fact, renowned researcher Dr. George Barna has found through extensive surveys measuring against seven core principles foundational to a biblical worldview that only 4 percent of Americans actually view their world through a biblical lens.[8]

What complicates matters is that our worldview is largely developed during childhood. Dr. Barna, Senior Research Fellow for the Center for Biblical Worldview at Family Research Council, has determined that a person's worldview is primarily established between the ages of fifteen months and thirteen years.[9] The problem is that the vast majority of kids reach their teenage years without a biblical worldview.

Here is more definitive evidence. The Nehemiah Institute, founded in 1986, is on a mission to provide worldview assessment to youth in Christian homes associated with Christian schools, homeschool associations, and church youth groups.[10] Called "PEERS," it is the only professionally validated worldview assessment available that I'm aware of. It's fairly comprehensive with seventy test items, fourteen in each category, that the kids take, and it breaks down the results. All the students who take the test fall into four broad categories of worldview:

- Biblical Theism (meaning a Biblical Worldview)
- Moderate Christian
- Secular Humanism
- Socialism

Keep in mind that this is only self-described Christian kids in Christian schools, youth groups, or homeschool. Based on almost forty years of results, PEERS testing shows that a majority of youth from Christian homes are abandoning a biblical worldview and biblical theism in favor of a secular worldview, if not a socialist worldview. When PEERS was first launched in the 1980s, the majority of youth from Christian homes scored mainly in either the moderate Christian worldview or biblical theism worldview. Today, the same demographic shows more than 90 percent of Christian youth scoring in the secular humanism category using the exact same questions that were used in the 1980s, and less than 3 percent are scoring in the biblical theism category. Again, these are kids in Christian schools, church youth groups, and homeschool.

Consequently, this is arguably the single greatest problem facing families and the church in America today, and why we must teach our children. We should not be surprised by these numbers when we are outsourcing the education of our children to people who, for the most part, not only don't have a biblical worldview, but many have an antibiblical worldview. This is why Scripture tells parents that we are primarily responsible to talk about God's Word with our children "when you sit in your house, when you walk by the way, when you lie down, and when you rise up" (see Deut. 6:4–9). We should be teaching our children and our grandchildren the Word of God and its application to our world. Yet when we outsource that to someone else, we see sad results. Of course, we must factor in that it is not simply what's happening in a classroom; it is also shaped by what they're listening to, watching, and engaging with on social media, etc. Furthermore, parents cannot give what they don't have. So, if parents don't have a biblical worldview, they cannot give their children a biblical worldview. And you cannot get a biblical worldview unless you are regularly reading the Word of God.

That brings me to the proposed solution. Again, to gain a biblical worldview, a person must be regularly reading and studying and applying the Word of God. That is what spurred me to develop our Stand on the Word Bible Reading Plan. It is a two-year, chronologically prioritized Bible reading plan that takes ten to fifteen minutes a day of reading, six days a week, Monday through Saturday. On Sunday, there's no reading because it's a discussion day for the family, a day to reflect on what we have read over the previous week and share how God is speaking to us.

This Bible reading plan came about a number of years ago when I was looking for a devotional book for our family—something that would allow five children, ranging from two to eighteen years old, to have a conversation. A lot of people send me books and devotionals with an interest in being a guest on *Washington Watch* to talk about their book, so I had a good handle on pretty much everything that was out there. I looked for six months—read them, studied them, went through them myself—and couldn't find anything that I felt would work. Finally, the Holy Spirit said, "Try the Bible."

So, we began with a couple of books from the New Testament, letters of Paul, and then I began to look at how we could take the entire Bible, breaking it up into a two-year reading plan as opposed to a one-year plan. The latter, for most people, becomes like a speed reading course where not much gets absorbed. However, with the two-year plan, everyone can read it in bite-sized chunks, and each day comes with two questions for reflection. The questions also served as an accountability to gauge who in the family was reading the chapters. And wherever I might be in the world, I would set my clock so that at 7 a.m. central time I would text my family the reading for the day and the two associated questions.

Then on Sunday, after lunch, we would have a conversation about the chapters we read that week and how it applies to the world in which we live. Our weekly time together as a family became the highlight of my week. Here is a suggested template for your gathering:

- Opening Prayer – Praise and a brief prayer for spiritual insight and unity.
- Recap – Briefly summarize the chapters covered that week.
- Discussion Questions – Use open-ended, age-appropriate prompts to spark meaningful worldview conversations. Here are some suggestions:
    1. Most meaningful passage that spoke to you personally?
    2. Insights gained about God: Who He is, What He values and expects, How He works?
    3. Applications that we can make from the Word to what is happening in the world?
    4. How would God have you apply His truth to your life personally?
- Action Steps – Encourage each family member to share a personal takeaway or action step for living the truth revealed in God's Word.

- Closing Prayer – Conclude by praising God for how He has revealed Himself, His purposes, and His ways, and by praying for His help in living in the light of His truth and sharing it with others during the week ahead.

For our family, these Sunday gatherings were nearly as meaningful as a church worship service! Now that nearly all of our kids are grown and some are establishing their own families, I pray they will do the same with their children as God gives them. But that was the strategy we used, and God has blessed it.

That Sunday debrief time is a key part of this strategy to develop a biblical worldview. The inspiration for it came about from a trip I took a number of years ago to Israel and attended a Shabbat dinner with a family. I was fascinated with the conversation around the dinner table, talking about the application of God's Word to the world in which we live. And I thought, "You know, that is what's missing, a conversation to help develop a biblical worldview." I had one child who was in college at the time. So, on Sunday we would dissect what they were being taught (because it was a secular college) and equip them to counter those arguments that they were hearing. We were honing her biblical worldview.

The bottom line here is that it is vitally important that we are intentional about cultivating a biblical worldview in our family members as well as with church members. I believe that reading the Bible daily, with a daily touch-of-base about the reading, followed by an extended weekend conversation can provide the solution to the challenge of making sure our families and our churches develop a biblical worldview. I pray you will join us on this Stand on the Word journey through the Bible. Visit frc.org/Bible to sign up or simply download the Stand Firm app.

Notes

1. "Daily Devotional: Can anything separate you from God?," Love Worth Finding, April 5, 2019, https://www.lwf.org/daily-devotions/can-anything-separate-you-from-god.

2. "Eight Words That Can Transform Your Life," Dale Carnegie Way, March 11, 2013, https://www.youtube.com/watch?v=l9ShWmhmraw.

3. Maureen Callahan, "Our greatest public health crisis? The angry young American male," *New York Post*, May 25, 2022, https://nypost.com/2022/05/25/our-greatest-public-health-crisis-the-angry-young-american-male/.

4. Michael Gryboski, ed., "YouVersion reveals top Bible verse for 2024," December 2, 2024, https://www.christianpost.com/news/youversion-reveals-top-bible-verse-for-2024.html#:~:text=Last%20year%2C%20YouVersion%20announced%20that,in%202022%2C%202020%20and%202018.

5. Henry H. Halley, *Halley's Bible Handbook: Classic Edition* (Zondervan, 2000), 816.

6. See John Knox, *Philemon Among the Letters of Paul* (The University of Chicago Press, 1935), 56–57.

7. https://research.lifeway.com/2021/09/09/christians-dont-share-faith-with-unchurched-friends/

8. Tracy Munsil, "Barna, CRC: Widespread Worldview Confusion Grows as Americans Redefine God," Arizona Christian University, February 18, 2025, https://www.arizonachristian.edu/2025/02/18/awvi-2025_01_most-americans-believe-in-a-supreme-power-but-not-the-god-of-the-bible/.

9. Tracy Munsil, "Most US Kids Ages 8-12 Lack Biblical 'Cornerstones,' Research Says," Arizona Christian University, October 11, 2023, https://www.arizonachristian.edu/2023/10/11/most-us-kids-ages-8-12-lack-biblical-cornerstones/.

10. https://www.worldviewcheckup.org/.

Other Study Guides Available from
Fidelis Publishing and Family Research Council

STAND on the WORD

Joshua: Finish Strong! ISBN: 9781956454802
Nehemiah: Rebuilding a Nation ISBN: 9781956454468
Jeremiah: Courage in a Cancel Culture ISBN: 9781956454369
Daniel: Visions and Valor ISBN: 9798992418651
Matthew: The King and His Kingdom ISBN: 9798992418682
Ephesians: Keep Standing! ISBN: 9781956454659

Also from Fidelis Publishing
and Family Research Council

STAND on the WORD Journals

Volume 1
ISBN: 9781956454758

Volume 2
ISBN: 9781956454871